HENCO

www.henco.com.mx
www.simoncohens.com

FULFILLED

FULFILLED
*The secrets of an entrepreneur who, in search of **success**, found **happiness.***

Tack Boutique
Editorial Director: Daniela Clavijo
Art Director: Lorenzo Cobos
Design and Production: Gerardo Castillo
Editorial Team: Mariela Gómez Roquero, Ximena Soto, Verónica Gonsenheim and Elizabeth Palacios
Style Correction: Alexandra Jardine Wall and Germán Sánchez

Tack Boutique S.A. de C.V.
Colima 161, Colonia Roma Norte,
Alcaldía Cuauhtémoc, C.P. 06700
Ciudad de México
www.tack.mx

First edition published in Mexico, 2021

ISBN: 978-607-29-2743-8
Printed in Mexico

FULFILLED

*The secrets of an entrepreneur who, in search of **success**, found **happiness.***

FULFILLED

ACKNOWLEDGMENTS

SIMON COHEN

On October 6th, 2020, the editorial team and I had our last meeting. FULFILLED was finished, and the excitement was indescribable. We were preparing for our big launch. That night, we slept happily, satisfied with the work accomplished.

At 4:18 AM the phone rang – that call you don't ever want to receive. My brother Pepe asked me to come to my parents' house. At 11:08 AM my dad passed away, after a year-long struggle with very aggressive brain cancer.

From the bottom of my heart, I dedicate this book to my father, Don Salomón Cohen, who gave me life and taught me to live FULFILLED. I share with you, reader, the farewell letter that I wrote with deep sorrow and profound admiration for him.

Dad:

You and I often said that the day we are born is the day we start dying. That the price we have to pay to live is to die. That the price we have to pay for loving is to suffer. And the deeper this pain is, the more immense the love for the one who goes.

Today, I thank life for this immense pain I am experiencing, because it shows the infinite love I have for you.

Today, we are heartbroken from so much love for you, but with our souls full of gratitude for everything you gave us and everything you leave us with.

Your passing has been the most difficult moment of my life. My hero is gone, my greatest example is gone, the person who gave me life is gone, the one who taught me to live it fully and with righteousness and firm values is gone.

Dad, I want to be like you! Because you taught me to be happy. You knew how to lead and listen. Together with my mom, you knew how to shape us into a family, and today we are more united than ever thanks to that.

Dad, I want to be like you! Because I learned to learn from you. You always expected us to keep improving ourselves and to grow constantly, and today, from the bottom of my heart, I thank you and I promise you that I'll continue this for the rest of my days.

Dad, I want to be like you! Because you always taught me to look ahead, to dream. You always told us: "Dream big because from there, the life of your dreams will become reality."

I want to be like you! Because today, we mourn you not just as a family, but surrounded by all the people whose lives you touched with your advice, with your smile, with your generosity.

I want to be like you! Because, through your example, you taught me to help others selflessly.

I want to be like you! Because you humbly taught us how someone can change and evolve based on mutual respect.

Dad, I want to be like you! Because you gifted your eternal smile to anyone who crossed your path.

I want to be like you! Because you always taught us that material things come and go, but when it comes to love, the more you give, the more you get.

Dad, I want to be like you! Because the day my grandchildren are born, I want them to see and admire me as yours admire you.

I want to be like you! Because you taught us that you can never leave a brother alone.

Dad, I want to be like you! Because the day my sons-in-law come along, I want them to love, respect, and admire me as your daughters-in-law do you.

I want to be like you! Because you gave everything to your friends without questions or conditions.

I told you this when you were alive, and I keep repeating it in my mind now that you are gone: you were the best father any human being could ask for. I cannot be more grateful to life for giving me the father I had. Every step, every word, every action reminds me of you. You were simply THE BEST!

I am grateful to life because it gave us a year to say goodbye and to tell each other so many things that we had not had the opportunity to speak about. We had time to talk, sing, laugh, and tell each other everything. Thank you for your wise advice! Those last lessons were the most significant because the circumstances were very difficult, and they came from the heart. Your legacy, your wishes, your will, I'll honor forever!

I regret nothing. I said it all to you when you were here, fully here.

Set a table for us in heaven, Daddy, because that's where we're all going, and when we meet, the party will be huge.

I'd give anything to have had you with us longer, but not in the condition you were in during your last months; not only were you suffering, but all of us who loved you suffered seeing you like that.

THANK YOU for being who you were! Now that you're gone, our hearts will be together forever. I will have to get used to not hearing your voice, to not being able to embrace you in my arms but instead with my soul, to not being able to look into your eyes and tell you things with words, but instead talk to you in my thoughts.

Not a day will go by that I don't think about you and how much I miss you.

Look out for me from above, watch me at all times because I assure you that you will always be proud of me, my actions, and how we will take care of each other and stay together as a family.

Rest in peace, chief!

I love you and I will love you forever!

My mother, who educated us with values, motivated us with determination, and gave us the confidence to never fall.

You are an inspiration. You are pure inspiration.

You always think about others before you think about yourself, and that makes you the greater person.

Your example has been, is, and will be an inspiration to many.

I adore you, Mom.

To my wife, my life partner, who has always helped me bring out the best version of myself.

You and I know that I owe everything I am to you.

Your humility inspires me, your love motivates me, your presence exalts me.

Infinite thanks!

To Joanna, Yael, and Michelle, my reason for living!

I want to be the best example, and you are my main motivator.

There is no greater joy than being by your side.

Your love is the engine of my soul.

May life lead you to be fulfilled always.

Thank you for existing!

To my brothers, José and Daniel, who nature gave me and with whom I share the same blood.

Brothers by divine work, partners by choice, friends by conviction.

You are my heroes in flesh and blood.

Together forever!

Margie, Yael, Janet, Salomón, Rachel, Salomón, and Sophia, the affection I feel for you is incomparable.

ooo

To Don Nemo, my father-in-law, for his optimism and way of seeing life.

To Mrs. Alice, my mother-in-law, who passed on before us, being my most fervent fan. Even from heaven, she knows the feeling is mutual.

ooo

To Eduardo, Rodrigo, Ricardo, Emilio, and Eduardo, you taught me to understand life from another perspective, to analyze it at a distance, and to learn from my mistakes. You make me grow infinitely.

ooo

To Saúl, Ilanit, Nessim, Nicole, and Daniela, the family love and our friendship are eternal.

To Mauricio and Joan, you are the brothers that I chose to have.

ooo

Juan Carlos, friends who inspire like you inspire me are a treasure.

ooo

To all who were, are, and will be part of the Henco family, I thank you; you are the true main characters of this story.

ooo

To Manfred and Thomas, my mentors and friends. I thank life for making our paths cross. My eternal thanks for having trusted me since I was basically a child. You began this story.

FULFILLED

FULFILLED

PROLOGUE

Eduardo Garza T. Junco

SIMON COHEN

When Simon Cohen asked me to write the preface to his book **FULFILLED:** *The secrets of a businessman who, in his search for success, found happiness*, I felt extremely honored.

After reading the book straight through in one sitting, connecting to the sensitive fibers that make life feel alive, it is clear to me that my objective here is to tell you, dear reader, that you are about to begin one of those little literary gems that connect us with truths that we all know are necessary for happiness, but that the daily grind keeps hidden from view. It is required reading, for it helps us listen to ourselves through someone else's story.

In these moments when Simon is near the middle of his life, he chose to share his experiences with us – with his heart on his sleeve and with total transparency, two things which distinguish him as a person.

I've known Simon since we were teenagers. Accepting my own subjectivity, I admire in my good friend the immense natural talent that has led him to be a great businessman, a caring son and brother, a loving husband and father, a close and empathetic friend, and a citizen committed to others. This book is a monument to his sincere interest in serving others by sharing his experiences openly. Thank you, Simon, for having the courage to do so.

We all have a story to tell. However, there are some who with their specific qualities invite us to reflect and dream more intensely. Such is the case of what is written in these pages.

I once heard that an answer to an unspoken question is no answer at all. We all go through life facing our challenges, learning to question the why's and how's. And, every once in a while, we come across a good book or a good friend who gives us the precise explanation to the question that life has presented us with.

FULFILLED is full of stories, examples, lessons, and ideas that offer answers to many of the questions that we ask ourselves over the years as we walk through life.

What is the definition of success? What are the most important things in life? How should we deal with failure? What is the purpose of a business enterprise? And is death even more worth our attention than it seems? These are the kinds of questions that Simon Cohen alludes to in an amusing, simple, but profound way, full of wisdom. He approaches these questions with incredible lightness and joy, which are an intrinsic part of his personality.

Thank you, Simon, for sharing. May life continue to give you the opportunity to feel **FULFILLED** and may this book inspire others to go through life with the same desire to live and the ambition to find happiness that you convey to us in these pages.

Eduardo Garza T. Junco
Board President at FRISA Industrias
November 1st, 2020

FULFILLED

INTRODUCTION

Jack Hilu

SIMON COHEN

It is a pleasure and an honor to read this book that narrates Simon's story and his way of seeing life. Talking about Simon is easy for me because when I talk about someone I love so much, it's as if I'm talking about myself.

I want to express what I feel for Simon and what he has built within his company. Most notable is that under his leadership, Henco has received several awards for being a different kind of company – a company where people work happily.

But, how did he achieve all this? How did he manage to be such a joyful person, who truly enjoys helping others? Simon has that chip: he likes to see people be happy, to see them laugh, and he has been able to radiate this at Henco.

When I visit their offices, there is a notably different atmosphere starting from when you arrive at the reception desk. Everyone wears a smile and greets you sincerely. You sense a different mood. Once inside, you feel you are in a refuge from the aggressive and stressful world outside, which is not where we want to be. I schedule my visits to Henco for 30 minutes and end up staying for two or three hours. I don't want to leave.

What is the recipe for doing what Simon does? How can a person spread his generosity to all those who cross his path? How can a person sow in his heart this love for people?

I am a fervent student of books written by great sages thousands of years ago, such as Maimonides, King

Solomon, and Moshe Chaim Luzzatto. These writers wanted to unravel the secret to having a fulfilled life, and my conclusion is that to be a better human being, one must always consider these five principles:

1. Occupy yourself with always doing good for others. The concept of giving generates empathy and affection for both the giver and the receiver. It is a virtuous circle.

2. Communicate with people in a friendly way, with respect, with honor, and always be the first to say hello.

3. Listen to people. When someone has a concern, let them talk about it. Why? Because knowing that someone is listening to you gives you comfort, it heals you, and helps you get through it.

4. Always greet people with a smile and a friendly face. Even if you don't give them anything else, if you offer them a smile, they're going to feel like you gave them a great gift.

5. Surround yourself with people better than you, from whom you can learn. Get together with good, honorable, fair, righteous people, because being close to them, their good values are infectious.

That's Simon Cohen, that's Henco. They hold dear and practice these principles: they always care about people's wellbeing; they always speak with respect and honor, the first to say hello; they're willing to listen and always greet everyone with a smile. To be close to Simon is to receive peace, tranquility. It is to be inspired by an honest, charismatic, correct person. He has a great gift for transmitting these principles.

Hopefully, after reading this book and understanding its concepts, each of us will be able to feel FULFILLED.

Jack Hilu
Mentor

FULFILLED

DAY **ZERO**

We have two lives: the second one begins when we realize we only have one.

SIMON COHEN
CAP 01

- Sir, it's your heart.

I heard the paramedic say these words in barely understandable English as soon as I woke up in the ambulance. Tammy, my wife, and Andy, my agent in China, were both at my side.

The paramedics insisted on taking me to a public hospital. Andy asked them to transfer me to St. Theresa's Hospital, one of the best in Hong Kong.

I was a world away from Mexico, where my three daughters were waiting for me: one was five years old, one was three, and the youngest was about to turn one. My parents and my brothers, my friends, my company, and a life I might never see again, were all thousands of miles away.

After that first diagnosis, and struck with the fear that has always been my Achilles' heel, my soul opened, and I felt it was important to tell Tammy a few things:

"Sweetie, you know how much I love you and will love you until the end of my days. I always tried to be a good husband, I always wanted to be a good human being, and give everything to you and our daughters. If I don't make it out of this, please tell them I love them and that I always will. Tell them that their father always tried to be an example of hard work, honesty, humility, and above all, love. I did my best to make a name for us. If I don't make it through this, I want you to live your life and to be happy."

At that point, we were both crying uncontrollably. I was 32 years old, and for the first time, I felt that the future was completely out of my hands. After so much hard work, trying by any means and at all hours to become a millionaire, I was not only facing the possibility of losing everything, but I would lose it while being far away from what was truly important.

When we arrived at the hospital and the paramedics had stabilized me, there was still a sensation of an electric shock running down my spine. The pain in my chest was still there, and the tingling in the muscles on my back was constant. It all happened so fast, from the moment I was taken out of the ambulance. They put us in a room that was suddenly filled with people. Some speaking in English and others in Chinese –they all sounded the same to me. They asked me my name, if I knew where I was, what year it was. The only thing I needed to know was what was going on, and whether or not my life was in danger.

They hooked me up to machines and did several tests, including an EKG. On a paper being printed out of the machine, I read the word 'abnormal' in the results. It confirmed what I had been told in the ambulance. I was afraid, terrified.

Once the tests were analyzed, the doctors delibera-ted about whether surgery would be necessary. Tammy, who always reacts better than I do in extreme situations, decided to call the father of a friend of ours who is a cardiologist –who has visited the cardiologist before the age of 32? As we spoke to the doctor in Monterrey, my anxiety increased and

Tammy, as always, was sober and calm in difficult times. She told him what had happened, explained that I had not slept well for several days, had not rested, exercised, or eaten properly, and that I had practically been working from sunrise to sunset for the last six days.

"From what you're telling me and what I'm seeing on the EKG, I'm almost certain your husband didn't have a heart attack. I think he has something called Wolff-Parkinson-White syndrome. People with this condition have an additional electrical pathway that causes the heart to beat much faster than normal and is sometimes mistaken for having a heart attack. He won't die from this. He needs to rest or he's going to end up destroying his body."

This pain was not foreign to me. When I was 17, at a national swimming championship just before I swam in the final heat of the 200-meter breaststroke, I went into the locker room and started the little ritual I had before an important competition: sitting down to meditate with my swimsuit on, a towel over my head, visualizing every stroke, every kick, the constant increase of my heart rate, the feeling of lactic acid in my muscles in the last meters of the race. That's when I first felt the shock like the one I felt in China. At that time, I had also lost consciousness for a while, only there was no one with me. It was never clear to me if I had fainted in the showers, and if so, for how long I had passed out. Regardless of how much time had passed, it was enough for me to miss the A-finals where I was supposed to compete against the eight best swimmers in Mexico.

I said goodbye to first place. I lost my shot at a national title because I didn't show up at the starting line. I was given the opportunity to swim in the B-finals, a chance at 9th to 16th place. The time I then clocked, even after this episode, was the best of my life up to that point. I would have won the gold medal if I had competed in the race I was supposed to. The sense of frustration was enormous; so big, that it overshadowed my locker room scare, and I never connected the episode to any kind of chronic problem. You feel invincible at that age, and even more so if you're a high-performance athlete.

My story as a swimmer began when I was very young, and it began not because of passion, but because of a doctor's orders. I was a sickly child, with asthma and all kinds of allergies. One day after I left the hospital, the doctor recommended swimming to my mother as the best remedy for my ailments. In those days no one would ask you, "What sport would you like to play, soccer, karate, gymnastics, tennis?" Medical instructions were followed to a tee, without questions. That's how I became a swimmer.

It's interesting how we often don't grasp the weight of every decision made throughout life, from those made for you by your parents when you're a child, to those you own up to as an adult. They are all connected and are paving the way to what some call 'destiny', and which I prefer to call 'lifelong learning'.

Each experience, each chosen path will yield a result, and even if sometimes it is not the expected one, it is possible to learn a new lesson. As one of my favorite phrases goes:

When you get what you want, it is life directing you. When you don't get what you want, it is life protecting you.

I owe a lot to swimming. I learned to detect and control anxiety, my great weakness, which along with fear is my biggest 'factory defect'. It allowed me to earn the scholarship with which I studied my undergraduate degree at Tec de Monterrey, one of the best universities in Mexico. There, I met best friends and life companions. It helped me to build my character in such a way that I was able to see and accept the fact that my time as a swimmer was over, and I managed to forge a new path for myself to become the Simon I am today. Finally, and most importantly, it was through swimming that I met my wife on the other side of the world. We'll get into that in a bit.

Even though I have never been the tallest nor the strongest, little by little, and thanks to tenacity, discipline, a winner's mentality, and drive that I inherited from my parents, I was able to get to first place. National champion on several occasions, Central American champion, national team for several consecutive years, until I came close to competing in the Atlanta Olympics in 1996. Failure to do so was one of the greatest frustrations of my youth, but it resulted in the opportunity to build the foundation of my life today. Everything happens for a reason, for something good, and we only come to understand this as time passes. These are gifts in disguise that life gives us.

The trip to China represented a turning point for me, from its very planning. Although I had been there several times, this visit to Hong Kong was particularly important because I was to meet personally with suppliers, shipping companies and agents. I had decided to go on this trip after my father, my brothers, and I agreed to buy the other half of the shares in our company from our German partners, with whom we had founded the international logistics company in 1998. Our specialty was ocean and air freight imports from East Asia to Mexico, as well as additional services to deliver customers' cargo in a timely and cost-effective manner. I would be introducing the new company to our longtime suppliers, and I was interested in the Chinese hearing from me in person in order to give them full assurance that they could trust us.

We were at the key moment where you either grow with a good transaction and move into the big leagues, or you stay small forever. It was May 2006, and for me it was a turning point as a businessman and I could not fail. The thought of the Olympic failure hung around my neck and here I had the possibility of a rematch, right in front of me.

I asked Tammy to come with me. In the last few years, we hadn't had enough time to be alone, just the two of us. She was dedicated fulltime to raising the girls, and I was focused on reaching what, until then, was my biggest goal: working like crazy, saving as much as possible in case of a crisis, and creating a solid, financially-sound future. I thought that achieving this involved certain sacrifices, including not having time with my daughters and missing out on their early years. The experience in China would be the beginning of an inner journey that led me to understand how wrong I was.

I've always believed that time is one of our most valuable assets, so when I traveled, I prepared activity-saturated schedules from start to finish. Not a minute's rest. Everything I could take advantage of, every minute, every second, every contact, and as many meetings as possible to get the most out of every business trip –I could come back as a tourist at some point in the future–. We landed in Hong Kong on a Sunday and the first appointment was on Monday at 7 AM. The combination of adrenaline and jet lag caused me to go days without sleeping.

Mornings started with breakfast with Tammy, then she would leave with a group of people whose job was to show her around the city. Meanwhile, I went from meeting to meeting with the directors of the most important shipping companies in huge and luxurious meeting rooms. Every time I walked into one of these rooms, I would say to myself, "What am I doing here? How did I get these important people to welcome me? I can't miss this opportunity!" Most of them were surprised to see me arrive without our German partners by my side, and every single time they asked me about my age –I seemed very young to them–. I showed up on time and well-dressed because, as they say: "In order to be someone important, first you have to look like someone important."

Duringeachappointment,Iexplainedourprojectindetail, and with all the confidence in the world, tried to convince the people across the table that we would be ta relevant player in the industry within a few years. I've always liked my work, and I consider one thing to be central when closing a good deal: people must be able to trust in what you say. The passion I had for doing things right and the desire to project total confidence to the people sitting across from me were qualities I possessed, and I knew it. In the end, our suppliers left with smiles on their faces, convinced that they were in good hands by staying with the new company, and that we would do great business together. I remember staying behind after these meetings had ended, watching the huge port cranes through the windows –the impressive ballet of shipping containers, and the efficiency with which they were loaded and unloaded in mere seconds–. I couldn't believe what I was experiencing. It was simply spectacular.

At the end of the day, we had dinner with some of the directors, who always attended to us impeccably, honoring the Asian tradition of making visitors feel important. When we returned to the hotel, I tried to sleep. Not one of those nights did I manage to sleep for more than two hours. I would work in the bathroom, sitting on the floor with my computer on my lap so as not to wake Tammy. I answered emails, talked to my team in Mexico, organized, operated, and took care of every last detail. During the day, I talked to the Chinese suppliers and agents; by night, with my people in Mexico. There were about 50 employees in the company then, all reporting to me. In my obsession to not fail and to give the best service during each shipment, all emails came and went CC'd to me: I didn't want to miss a single thing. I needed to be informed of and in control of absolutely everything. I felt successful, but what I didn't know was that

When 'success' comes at the expense of your health, your family, or your friends, it's not success.

I was as tired as I was motivated, and this kept me from hearing the alarm my body was sounding. On Friday morning, I woke up with a very strange feeling. My chest hurt and some kind of energy was running up and down my spine, as if an electric shock were coursing from my tail bone through the back of my neck and then down into my back muscles. My eyes were painful and irritated, and I showed symptoms of what could well be the onset of a cold. With so much going on, it was hard to tell if it was exhaustion or something else. Tammy suggested that we go downstairs and have breakfast, thinking that a hot coffee and a couple of aspirin would make me feel better. The schedule had to be followed. After all, it was Friday and the weekend would begin soon. We could sleep, rest, relax, and get back in shape to continue working first thing Monday morning.

And so, I kept at it with coffee and a couple of aspirin. By noon, I was back in the rhythm and in tune with my work, as if caffeine had given me a boost. That afternoon, we went by subway from our agent's offices in Hong Kong to Kowloon, where we had the last and most important meeting of the trip. The subway was full, bursting at the seams with passengers wearing suits and ties –everyone looked like executives from major companies. Very orderly, but each car was filled to maximum capacity.

Senior managers of the Japanese shipping company NYK (Nippon Yusen Kaisha) would honor us by taking us to a very special place, the Pacific Club, a sports and social club located in the old port overlooking the impressive buildings of the city and its spectacular night light show. To get to the club's entrance, you cross a shopping center filled with boutiques of the best international brands. Between my amazement at the beauty of the place and the anxiety about the important meeting, I again forgot about my symptoms. My body was begging for a bit of rest, but the adrenaline and the excitement of being in this place with the big boys kept me from feeling it.

We were on the terrace, waiting for the always-punctual Japanese to arrive, when I felt the same cramp from that morning running down my spine. Once... twice... "Sweetie, I'm not well." Tammy ordered a Coke, thinking my blood pressure had dropped. She told me to take a deep breath, and with a comforting tone, she reassured me that everything was fine, that a full day's rest was not far off. We went out to the balcony and the sight of Hong Kong was breathtaking. I was still feeling chest pain and electric shocks down my spine. We returned to the hall and from a distance, I saw our hosts arrive. When the first of them approached to greet me, I felt the first blow on my chest. Hard and solid, like when you get sucker punched. I sat down and feeling quite embarrassed, I apologized.

A few seconds later, when I tried to get back up, the second blow came. Stronger and more forceful than the first one, and I said to Tammy, "Sweetie, call an ambulance." Embarrassed, I walked to the bathroom. I don't remember anything else. They say I passed out. The paramedics took longer than usual to arrive because it was rush hour and it was difficult to access the site. Once on a gurney, Tammy running in high heels next to me and Andy more scared than ever, we crossed the mall until we reached the ambulance, the only way out of there.

After several days in the hospital, with the Wolff-Parkinson-White diagnosis confirmed, and too much stress, we decided to go to the hotel and spend a few more days there. We cancelled the remaining appointments. Tammy and I agreed that we would follow up with the cardiologist in Mexico. Little by little, I started taking meetings again. I was still not quite 'getting' what had happened and kept insisting on my rush to deliver, deliver, deliver. The trip was over. Our return flight was very long: Hong Kong - Taipei - Los Angeles - Monterrey. During the first leg, the only discomfort was not being able to sleep. I still felt weird, but I was fine.

While on the longest leg of the trip from Taipei to Los Angeles, Tammy fell asleep after we had eaten. Not long afterwards, I started to feel the same chest pain I'd had in the Pacific Club. My heart wouldn't stop. I estimated that it was beating about 200 times per minute –I had learned how to take my heart rate after my experience at the pools. I called the flight attendant over, and when she saw me, she immediately called the captain and activated the emergency protocol. Luckily, there was an American doctor on the plane who was coming home from vacation in Thailand. I explained what had happened in China and the diagnosis I had been given. If at ground level I had been distressed at not being able to control the speed of my heartbeat, the scenario looked much worse at 40,000 feet, and Tammy was sound asleep from the pills she had taken to rest during the long flight. I thought the diagnosis could have been wrong, and that my life was really in danger. "I will not get out of this one alive", I said to myself.

The doctor injected me with something that knocked me out for the rest of the trip. I remember nothing else. I don't even want to imagine what would have happened if the doctor hadn't been on that flight.

The first thing we did when we arrived at the airport in Monterrey was go straight to the hospital to see the same cardiologist who had given us his diagnosis by phone in Hong Kong, and he confirmed what he had said: Wolff-Parkinson-White, aggravated by intense stress. I was treated for a year to help with anxiety and control my heart rate. It was out of my control, which made me more anxious. I wanted to rest and eliminate stress, but trying to unplug from work made me more anxious. I was in an endless vicious circle.

That's when one of the most important revelations in my life as a businessman struck: I had to learn to delegate what I used to do, to understand that not everything could –nor should– depend on me, and I began to treat my illness at its root. Therapies, psychiatrist, psychologist, cardiologist, and a considerable number of medications. I began to do meditation and tried to slowly get back into sports. I tried various techniques to sleep better and learned to eat properly, in a very healthy way. I understood that these activities are essential to having a good life.

I also made things right with my family: buying the company from the German partners generated friction between us and, for the first time, our healthy relationship had been jeopardized. I knew that in addition to stress, this issue was a major burden on my heart; it had to be fixed, and the only way to achieve this was by talking and reconciling. I didn't know how –listening to others wasn't my strength. To get my family back I had to learn. We all had to learn.

I decided to devote my energy to building, not to destroying and fighting. Life gives us a limited amount of energy each morning and we have the right to choose how and to what ends we use it. In fighting and being destructive, or in building and being creative. It's our choice.

The personal lessons from this experience made me think about what I wanted from my life. I was 33 years old and taking a lot of medicine, including a couple of anti-anxiety drugs that made me feel like a rag doll. I confessed to Tammy that I hadn't felt well for a year, that I needed a reboot. I wanted to connect with nature and disconnect from technology and work. I didn't need more hours of light sleep –it was my soul that was tired. A good laugh and deep sleep cure everything, I thought. I needed peace, nature, freedom. I urgently needed quality time with my daughters and my wife, to be still for a moment without worrying. I was in urgent need of an awakening of the spirit, to start living again.

We agreed to go somewhere far away, without an internet connection and surrounded by natural beauty. The goal was to gradually give up the anti-anxiety medication and spend two weeks as a family, with peace and surrounded by love.

We rented a little house on the beach, no internet, no computers, no distractions. The sea was crystal clear.

We could walk hundreds of feet from the shore and the water would only reach up to our knees. There were starfish everywhere you looked. There was no human noise at all. The compound had only 12 houses, tastefully decorated, and equipped to make you feel very comfortable, away from everything. Because it was off season, only three homes were occupied, and the service was impeccable.

From the moment we arrived, the view of that endless, calm, and transparent sea captivated us. Merely 30 feet separated our balcony from the sea. We immediately ran to get our feet wet in the water. It was the perfect place to be –truly be– the five of us together.

Our daily routine was extraordinary. I would wake up before everyone else and work out. When I got back, we'd make breakfast together and play with the girls for a while. We would go to the beach, play, eat, and then keep playing... then take a nap. Wake up and watch the sunset: the sky painted orange with hypnotizingly beautiful blue stripes, the clouds turned pink, a riot of color reflected in the turquoise sea. Dinner and a boardgame before going to bed. Eating healthy, sleeping well, and exercising are the perfect recipe for rebooting our bodies.

On the fifth night, after dinner the power went out. We were in complete darkness. My girls were scared, so I decided that the five of us should go outside to the beach to lie down on the sand and look at the stars. It was the most beautiful sky I had ever seen, with thousands of stars, you could even see the Milky Way! Shooting stars surprised us and made us smile, and we'd make bets on who could spot the most. My daughters stretched out on my belly, and I put my head on Tammy's legs. We were looking for shapes in the sky: a Mickey Mouse, a horse, a mermaid. And there, with the greatest treasure a human being can imagine, already back to feeling like myself, I finally felt an enormous sense of peace.

In that moment, I was the happiest and luckiest man in the world. I started crying and finally let go of the fear of death that had accompanied me since childhood and that had been worsened by the terrible experience in Hong Kong.

– "Why are you crying, Daddy?"
– "I'm crying because I'm happy."

Looking up at the sky and hugging my daughters with all my might, I told them: "I'm crying because I'm afraid. I'm crying because I don't know how much longer I'll be alive. Nobody knows! I'm crying because I love you guys deeply and would like to enjoy my life more. Girls, I promise you that starting today I will try to be the happiest man in the world. Nothing and nobody will stop me from doing this! I will truly appreciate what is actually important: my health, my family, my friends. I love you and I want you to remember that. What we are experiencing right now is the most valuable thing there is: being together. Every day we must be grateful for what we have and also for what we don't have. This moment is magical. This is being happy."

That night, Tammy and I talked for hours. Of what had happened, of what was to follow. Of our life as a couple, as parents, as our parents' children. How we would honor our parents and live hand-in-hand with our siblings, with all our differences, flaws, and virtues. Accepting that what is different from our way of thinking in fact complements us and makes us better. How we were going to be such good friends. We talked about transcending.

We connected again, made agreements. From that day on, I decided that I was going to be the best example of what we had talked about that night on the beach, and that every day I was going to be grateful for the opportunity to be here and now. My daughters would no longer have an absentee father who worked so that they would not lack money. No more power struggles to decide what was for whom. It became clear to me that happiness was the only way to achieve my personal and professional goals, and if along the way I helped more people do the same, then I could consider myself a successful man.

I met with my dad and my brothers. We were in constant disagreement about the business at that time. I told them what had happened to me, and we agreed to be at peace. "Sometimes, it's better to be at peace than to be right", I thought. We must use our energy to build, and together be an unwavering force that would transcend forever.

Back in the office, I sat down with my closest collaborators and told them: "Today you will meet a new Simon, a Simon who has thought things through and decided to be happy. To do this, I have to be surrounded by people who want what I want. From now on, I will put all my effort and dedication towards kindling the right conditions for this to happen. I want to walk alongside as many people as possible towards a good life, surrounded by love and happiness."

It was teamwork, and a new philosophy had to guide us, focused on individual and shared happiness. I wanted those of us who worked at Henco to come to the office every day with a smile on our faces, and when things weren't going well in someone's life, I wanted us to have a strong team there to support them and help them get through it. To be happy is also to have a good support system, and in that sense, I've been a millionaire since I was born.

We came into this world to be happy. The problem is that we forget. I don't know a single person who when asked if they want to be happy answers, "No, my goal in life is to be bitter and to suffer." Our pace of life is very fast: it makes us worry about shallow things that eventually become important, and then, what is really important becomes shallow.

Life is a long path full of problems, and that is why we come to this world: to solve problems! We can do it in two ways: frowning, irritated, and angry, or with love, smiles, and believing that everything is for the best. With faith, with inner peace.

One of my favorite words is 'ataraxy' because it perfectly defines what I had been looking for ever since the two incidents I describe at the beginning of this book. It is a philosophical term to describe keeping our emotions balanced by seeking inner peace: a peaceful state of mind, where pain and fear are absent.

Even before what happened in Hong Kong, and for as long as I can remember, I lived in fear of the future, believing that being at peace meant having all material needs satisfied.

Your happiness today cannot depend on something that happened in the past or will happen in the future.

Children are happy because they don't worry about what has already happened or what is to come, they concentrate all their energy on living in the present.

What happened in Hong Kong in 2006 forced me to look inward and live every day being grateful for what I have, what I don't have, and above all, for all the people around me. That's how my 'day zero' happened, the day that my life began again. A **FULFILLED** man lives intensely and is ready to transcend at any moment. That's how I lost my fear, my anxiety, and decided to enjoy 'my second life', **FULFILLED!**

FULFILLED

THE ART OF
SLEEPING PEACEFULLY

Happiness is the new rich,
inner peace is the new success,
health is the new wealth, and
education, respect, and values are
the base for our future.

SIMON COHEN
CH 02

Having decided to be a happy man has been one of the most pivotal points in my life. It was undoubtedly a moment of change, of breaking with much of what I had done in the past, focused only on meeting my financial goals, without rest, without pause, and in such a hurry.

There are two types of dreamers: the first one dreams in his sleep, at night; the second dreams during the day, and at night he can't sleep. That yearning that goes round and round in your head. I was the second type, I became obsessed.

When the failure of my Olympic dream was confirmed, I turned to my father to open the doors of the family's textile business to me, and do my part in a time of economic crisis –1996– when there was a huge need for foreign currency to pay off the company's debts. In May of that year, I graduated with a bachelor's degree in International Trade, and without experience, only recently graduated, I was the person best suited to start exporting the factory's products.

Together with my brother, Pepe, who had been helping my father in the business for some time, we realized that there was a huge gap in the service provided to us by the international freight companies, shipping companies, and forwarders that supplied us. It was almost impossible to have a call with them that lasted less than 30 minutes. Nobody provided information nor was interested in answering us. We were too small to get their attention.

One day, while talking to Pepe, we dreamed of starting an international logistics business and providing a high-quality service to small and medium-sized companies that were not being properly attended to. We already had some suppliers, and the one we felt most comfortable with was Cargo Masters International, a German-Mexican company, whose owners, Manfred and Thomas, would become my future partners, mentors, and great friends.

"How are you doing, Simon?", Manfred said very nicely on the phone one of the first times I spoke to him. After talking for a few minutes, he asked me: "Do you remember our agent in Monterrey? Starting today, he is no longer an agent and now you can deal with everything directly with me for your next shipments."

I went crazy. Such an important person in the world of logistics was calling me, a 23-year-old boy, and opening the door to talk directly to him. Between my excitement and the dream that Pepe and I had talked about recently, I didn't want to end the call. A few minutes passed, and after saying goodbye, just before hanging up, having already taken the earpiece away from my head, I heard Manfred say: "Hey, by the way, let me ask you one more question: among the competitors who have visited you or your acquaintances, do you know anyone in Monterrey who is between 30 and 40 years old, speaks good English, knows about the industry, and has a good network?"

Now I really lost it.

Without thinking twice, I said, "Me! I'm 23 years old, I know nothing about the industry, but I can learn, I speak very good English, and I have many friends."

"You're very young and you have a family business to run. I don't think your profile is right", he replied.

I wanted to know when Manfred would come to Monterrey. He said in three weeks. "I will see you then, I'm going to set up an important schedule with appointments so we can get to know each other and talk more about this", I added immediately.

I didn't know who to turn to. I was facing an important opportunity and I had to act immediately and correctly. I wanted to surprise and impress Manfred, and I was on the clock. There's no second chance to make a first impression, I thought. I started calling all my friends.

As I sought them out, I was surprised to realize how many people I knew who were willing to help me. When Manfred finally arrived, I had an incredible contact list filled with my friends' parents and their network, which opened doors to the biggest companies in Monterrey to me, some of which even Manfred himself had not been able to get to before. He was so surprised and pleased with my performance that he offered me work for a few months.

I approached my dad and my brothers, and I told them what had happened. Their first reaction was not positive. "We need to add another pillar to this company, generate a new source of income." "Let me try, we won't lose anything if it doesn't work", I argued. In my mind, having this go wrong was not an option, so I started working at lightning speed.

The quality of my work was such that when the deadline was met, Manfred and Thomas offered to make us partners in a new business in Monterrey, Cargo Masters del Norte, which would eventually become Henco Global.

Manfred was my mentor, the man who helped me start this business and with whom we managed to grow very quickly. I am eternally grateful to him, for his knowledge, friendship, and guidance; his humility was for me the greatest example of what I wanted to be: every time we got into a car, he sat in the back seat so that I could sit up front; for every question I had, he explained the answer to me as many times as necessary, until I understood; in meetings, he gave me my place and introduced me as his partner; he never made me feel less important, on the contrary, he gave me importance, and this, in turn, made him look even greater. His calm and sensible way of analyzing the situations and problems we faced taught me that not everything in life is solved by shouting and insulting others. His formula was much better and more effective.

During the first meetings I went to with Manfred, I wrote down everything, absolutely everything, from the way he greeted people to the technical terms that I didn't yet know. Once the meetings were over and we were in the car, I asked him all the questions that came to my mind. He answered absolutely everything, with the patience that characterized him. I needed to learn how to sell, to do it properly when I was on my own.

We would make a summary of the meetings and he would explain to me the reasons behind each comment he had made.

He never left me on my own: we went hand-in-hand together in the small, medium, and large projects, we even chartered an Antonov-124 –the biggest plane in the world at that time– in the year 2000. With Manfred, I learned that nothing was impossible; if we could do this, we could achieve anything and compete with any multinational, regardless of its size.

Thomas was a great partner. In a direct and businesslike way, we talked endlessly about potential clients and the international companies we would conquer. We traveled many times together to Europe and Asia, and each time we learned from each other things that I still put into practice today. His authenticity made this time together very fun, and his knowledge of the industry made him a great teacher as well.

The company started growing quickly, and I was still dead set on the money: I wanted to be a millionaire. I kept thinking, "If someone else has done it, I can do it too. I won't stop trying", and I worked harder and harder each day.

I stopped sleeping well. Many days I skipped lunchtime, and I completely gave up exercise. I lived so close to my office that sometimes I'd take a 15-minute break to give my babies a bath and then I'd go back to get done what I'd left unfinished. My sole obsession was work.

The difference between pain and suffering is that pain is physical and suffering is produced in the mind. I started to suffer, and that's what we shouldn't allow to happen.

We hired a lot of people because we were growing at a steady pace, but I was suffering from it. From April 1998, when we started working in this independent company, until 2006, we managed to achieve a constant rate of growth, in double and triple digits. While the German partners were focusing on Europe, I decided that we had to position ourselves in Asia; that's when the exponential growth of China's exports to the rest of the world came along, and we were in the right place at the right time.

In 2005, Manfred, Thomas, Pepe, and I had talked about the possibility of joining forces and making a unified group, because the growth projections were huge. However, at the beginning of 2006, one of them told us that it would not be possible; there were many vested interests, and although our relationship was extraordinary, the merger would put what we had built so far at risk. The status quo was not an option, and after many hours talking with my dad and Pepe, we decided to buy or sell 50% of our stake in Cargo Masters del Norte.

We analyzed both options in depth and realized that the best thing to do was to buy our partners out. The company was run 100% by me, its potential would be diminished with my departure, and this was well understood by Manfred and Thomas. The trip to China where I had the 'incident' took place a few months later, in May. By that time, we were already openly discussing the idea of them selling us their shares. 2006 and 2007 were very complicated years, in which I lived immersed in stress. June 2007 was the trip to the beach with my family, and four months later, we closed the deal and negotiated keeping 100% of the shares. In December 2008, we renamed the company Henco Global, a name born from the syllables of our surname: CO-HEN, HEN-CO.

Since mid-2007, I was clear about what was coming in 2008, achieving the business's liftoff would be very important. I had sown the seeds for this success, I was cultivating it, and I wanted to reap the harvest: we would achieve exponential growth.

If we were slow to buy the company, the numbers would be different, and the value would also be very different. We had to act immediately: timing was everything. Negotiating the price was no longer the most important thing –we were at an amount between the number they were asking for and what we were willing to pay– even though we knew we had no money, we would take it out of the cash flows. The important thing now was to close the deal before the end of 2007.

It was October 25th and Manfred had to travel to Germany, and, he'd be away for more than a month to deal with his business and personal affairs. "Let's close the deal before you leave", I said. "No, when I get back", he replied. I knew that if he left without closing the deal, we'd have to start negotiations all over again when he came back. I took the first flight to Mexico City and arrived at their offices at 4 PM. After greeting each other affectionately and chatting for a few minutes, we got straight to the negotiation. We thanked each other for almost 10 years of working together and promised that, whatever the outcome, our friendship and esteem for each other would remain intact. The noise of people talking outside the conference room was increasing because it was the end of the day, and that's when I realized I needed to start nailing down the agreement. It was crunch time.

As I was about to touch upon the main issue, the electricity went out. It was already starting to get dark outside. I couldn't believe it. Manfred asked me to continue the conversation another day. I wasn't willing to let my plans be ruined, so I convinced Manfred and Thomas to keep going. I accepted the last price they had put on the table and focused on negotiating the terms: credit for one year.

They accepted the proposal and I gave them each a small bank check to seal the deal. You can't make a bad deal with good people. Manfred and Thomas are good people. Manfred came back in mid-December and we made the formal contract and the share purchase. From that day on, my dad, Pepe, and I began to plan differently, everything from long-term goals to how to get my brother Daniel, who had just graduated from college, involved in the business.

In 2008, the term they had given us came due, and we paid for the shares on time using the cash flow from the business. We achieved our goal with the whole team's extraordinary effort. The sellers were satisfied with what they had charged, and we were happy with the way we had been able to pay it: a real win-win. Our strategy was so successful that in 2011, London Business School, one of the best business schools in the world, wrote a case study about it for undergraduate, Master's, and executive education students.

On the family front, when we returned from China and while I was trying to regain my health, family problems and arguments took on darker overtones as the pressure to make decisions and buy the German partners' shares grew. How would we distribute the new shares, who would be the new owners, and with what percentages?

There was a difference in opinion between my brothers, my father, and me, which added to the stress of running the company. This, in addition to the fact that at that time I had no contracts in China to increase my load and my promises to customers could not be broken. It was now or never!

On the beach, my vision changed. I did want to take the company to the next level, but I had made a firm decision to be a happy man, and to achieve that I needed peace. The first step was to sleep peacefully. I had to stop arguing with my family and reconcile.

Once we had acquired the other 50% of the company, we decided to get my brother Daniel involved, and he has since become an invaluable part of the team. A lot of people who knew about this criticized me openly and harshly. Today, I am grateful that I had that clarity, even though it took me a couple more years to reach a final agreement with my brothers and my dad.

When I look at it now, I feel like I couldn't have been more right. I had to feel death near to understand that there are things in life that are more important than material things, as the saying goes: "There are people so poor, so poor, that all they have is a lot of money." I didn't want to be a lonely millionaire with no family.

In no way am I saying that you can live without money; on the contrary, generating wealth helps us hire more people and generate well-being for them and their families. You can't be happy while hungry or cold, it is what it is.

I understood that together, we would be an unbeatable force and our differences would be our strengths, that we were a great team because we complemented each other. I was not wrong: together, we have done things that I would never have achieved on my own.

Today, my personal and business philosophy is "High Performance, Happy People", because you are more likely to find happiness if you are a high achiever than if you are a lazy person who doesn't want to do anything. If you are unemployed and have no money, no house or shelter, if you have nothing, it's going to be very difficult to be happy. If you have financial stability and peace, it will be easier to enjoy a full life. It's very complicated to find happiness within oneself, but it is impossible to find it anywhere else.

Heaven and hell are not physical places: they are states of mind. When you're at peace, you're in heaven; when you're not, you're in hell.

It is worth asking ourselves what really matters: money, family, or the love of the people around us? I think it's a balanced mix of everything. Aren't there bitter people who have a lot of money, or happy people who are not wealthy? What about those who have lost their family for money? Is it worth it?

Our goal in life should be constant growth in all aspects: intellectually, economically, in friendships, love, and family. The day you stop growing is the day you start dying, so I consider life to be a permanent process of learning and maturing.

Let's think about it this way: if money is infinite, and you think it's the only thing that's going to give you happiness, then happiness is going to be unattainable. The day you achieve your first goal, you're already looking for the next one. We always work for a better tomorrow, but when that tomorrow comes, instead of enjoying it, we again think of a better tomorrow. Let's have a better today and enjoy the present! People who have less do find happiness in meeting their basic needs, but there is a point where material things can bring problems. You can avoid this by balancing the scales.

Back from the beach, when I talked to my team at the company and shared my feelings with them, we decided to work on three aspects that are fundamental for any person:

- **Wellness:** sleeping well, eating well, and exercising.
- **Mindfulness:** meditation, peace of mind, and gratefulness.
- **Happiness:** enjoying life, family, friends; giving and inspiring.

The sum of these three actions will result in us becoming high performers. If we did this, we would reach our goals faster and, at the same time, our quality of life would improve. Thus was born the philosophy that today is a fundamental part of our company: High Performance, Happy People.

To know that you did your best is to be at peace, to come home and sleep in harmony. You can't be at peace if you don't do your job well. Tranquility is the greatest manifestation of happiness. It's that easy.

We have to be aware that when we fall into the depths, it is because down there, there is something to be found, something to be learned.

It is clear to me today that no one can choose the day they'll die, but we do have the ability to decide what attitude we will face life with. I did a full analysis of how I wanted to live because in my mind the countdown had started: how many vacations did I have left with my daughters and Tammy? How many visits to my parents, how many get-togethers and parties with friends? Realizing that there were few, I decided to enjoy every aspect of each day to the fullest.

We don't have another chance! Life is not a rehearsal! It's real, it's a one-off. Let us be happy, not because everything is perfect or fine, but because we are alive and that is reason enough to celebrate.

There is no life without obstacles; we cannot find an easy and obstacle-free existence with a straight and level path. We are going to encounter pebbles –or boulders– along the way. That is life! We came into this world to enjoy ourselves, and along the way, we have to solve problems. There's no choice. Everyone, without exception, no one is spared. Everyone! A positive attitude helps us see the difficulties as smaller obstacles, but if we see them in a negative way, they will seem impossible to overcome. I insist:

One is not happy because everything is fine, but because one finds the good in everything.

Throughout my life, I've realized that all people suffer, it's like an instinct! The rich suffer because they are rich, and the poor because they are poor; the fat guy because he is fat, and the thin guy because he is thin. The neighbor's garden always looks greener. This causes us unnecessary suffering.

We have to value and love everything that is ours. Whether it is a lot or a little, it is ours!

Remember when you yearned for what you have today? That's how it's always going to be; constant growth!

Happiness is the difference between your expectations and your reality, between what you want and what you have. The more aligned they are, the happier you are and the less frustrations they cause. Hand in hand with constant intellectual, moral, professional, and spiritual growth. That's how peace happens.

The more you work for something, the more you enjoy it when you get it. If you can go home and sleep soundly, congratulations! You're much closer to happiness than you might have imagined.

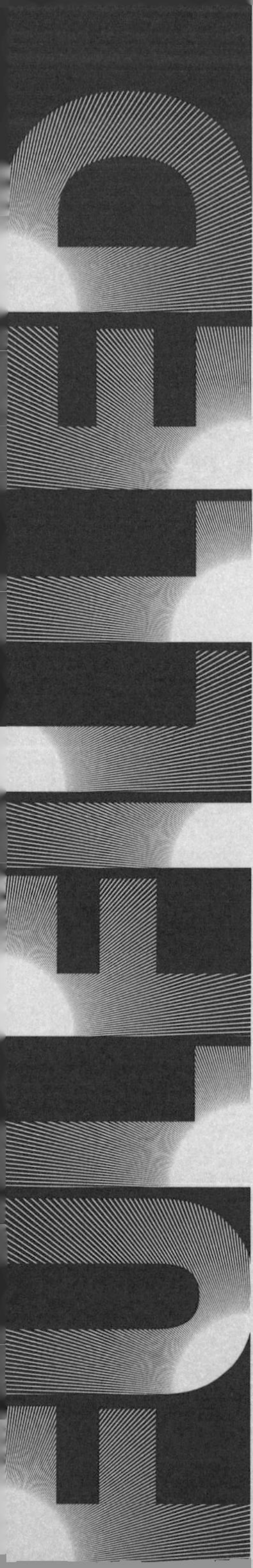

EYES ON THE STARS, **FEET ON THE GROUND**

Strive to be so great that everyone wants to be like you, and so humble that everyone wants to be with you.

SIMON COHEN
CH 03

Ever since I learned to see life differently, from another angle, and focusing on others before thinking about myself, I began to feel at peace.

When nothing changes, if I change, everything changes.

I took refuge in this sentence and, indeed, it happened. I was motivated and truly committed to the promise I had made to the four most important women in my life. I knew that I had to start putting into practice what my mind visualized as the second part of my life.

The responsibilities didn't stop, everything kept going. But what had happened a year before, and the way my team at Henco closed ranks to support me, to keep us afloat, and to take care of the company, made me realize once again that I was surrounded by incredible human beings. I knew I was very lucky.

What until then had seemed like a success story was actually creating a sense of emptiness in me, and I wanted to stop feeling that way. But what was causing this in me? What was the trigger of this apparently unfounded anguish, and why did I feel incomplete? A few months earlier, we had closed an excellent deal to buy the shares from our German partners, and the company was already in my family's hands. The numbers showed growth, even though the global economy was going through a rough patch in 2009. I was surrounded by a spectacular team that took care of me, my family, and Henco. Everything appeared to be fine.

However, few people imagined what was behind the 'successful' businessman who felt threatened by life itself, and who had set out to redefine his priorities.

I always wanted to succeed, have a business, earn money, and give work to many people. I knew that entire families depended on me achieving my goals. Failure was never an option. The idea of not doing well never crossed my mind, not because I felt invincible or thought I was the best, but because I was always afraid, and fear makes you humble.

On the day of my graduation from Tec de Monterrey, after receiving my degree, my father approached me. He congratulated me, then quietly uttered a phrase that he liked very much to say: "Strive to be so great that everyone wants to be like you, and so humble that everyone wants to be with you." One of the first lessons I learned is that I was vulnerable and therefore had to be humble.

Arrogance can be a dangerous companion. In fact, I am convinced that it is the main cause of death for companies, businesses and empires. I always tried to keep my feet firmly on the ground, although at times, it was a difficult thing to do. Ego taps you on the shoulder and, naturally, you begin to grow taller. You start believing that you are better than others. Nothing could be further from the truth. Your values, friends, and family are the ones that pull you back to Earth. There are people extremely capable in areas where you are weak, so it is important to learn from the people around you.

Nobody gives you anything in this life. If I wanted to achieve my dreams, I had to work hard and without neglecting my health. I had to try harder than others, give more than the rest to compete in the best way, and if there was something another company did better, use their example and learn from it. I have always had a lot of respect and admiration for my competitors, regardless of the size of their company.

I stand by the idea that we must protect our industry, not just our company. We must clearly define where we want to compete and where we can collaborate. We must defend the ecosystem, create a bigger market; if it grows, we will all grow and there will always be more opportunities. 50% of the biggest companies in the world have some kind of agreement to collaborate with their competitors. Why not do it ourselves?

At the time, and to this day, at Henco we do what is necessary to offer our clients the best service and we try to solve their problems. This became a way of life, a habit. Although we are not perfect, and our industry is unpredictable, the goal is to remove the hassle for our clients so that they can focus their energy where they create value.

Business, like everything in life, has its ups and downs. In my career as an athlete, I didn't achieve all my dreams. Although this can be considered a setback, today I know that I when fell down, I got up and learned. When you lose, don't miss out on the lesson. If there is a great teacher of life, it is failure. Setbacks are important if you are in the process of learning. The secret does not lie in falling down many times, but in getting up and coming away strengthened. We will mess up –not once, not twice, not three times... thousands of times!.

But you have to get up and keep piling on the lessons that every obstacle leaves you with. Fall a thousand times and get up a thousand and one.

When you think you've failed, stop for a minute and ask yourself: what is failure? It's not when you don't reach your goal; it's not reaching the goals and not learning from the experience –that's the real failure! Because, as Nelson Mandela, South African activist and politician, used to say: "I never lose; I win or I learn."

The next time you fall, get up, and remember that there are no failures; they're just paths and we're all walking down them.

When you're tired and don't want to go on, rest, but don't quit!

The stumbling and the perseverance will make you grow, and we've all been there. There is not a single successful person on the planet who has not stumbled many, many times. Truly, there isn't.

Being open to learning from failure does not mean giving up on being ambitious. On the contrary, ambition is good when it is well directed. If you just want to accumulate money, it's not ambition, it's greed. I won't deny that, maybe just like you, I dreamt of being a millionaire one day. I wanted to have a lot of money! What could be wrong with that? "When your mind is not in control, it is insatiable, like fire: it always wants more."

If I had already managed to become a competitive swimmer even without the optimal physical qualities, why couldn't I one day hold high rank as a businessman? If they can, I can! I was wondering what the secret was –working hard? I'm capable! Doing it smartly? That's how we do it! I realized that all of this could lead me to make a lot of money, but what I couldn't guarantee was whether I would be a happy person, because happiness is a combination of using your gifts, doing what you like in a disciplined way, and following the rules.

Doing the work you are good at and loving doing it every day –that is not work, it is joy.

And here is another lesson given to me during my time as an athlete. Without discipline, no one wins a competition nor builds a successful business. Without discipline, I wouldn't be able to care for my body, mind, and spirit, or teach my daughters integrity and values, or run a company where the most important thing is to solve problems for those who trust us.

If, in every failure you experience, you can learn and can be a better person, what does it mean to fail? For example, in sports. If we look at it abstractly, the truth is that I had the goal of going to the Olympics and I failed. If we look at the reality up close, I know I was a successful man and I'll explain why: being a high-performance athlete, discipline became a part of my being; I made best friends; I traveled around the world; I studied on a scholarship... and the list goes on. I'll tell you the most important result: thanks to swimming, I met my wife. Only after having chosen to do this sport competitively, could I have come to meet and then marry the woman who is today the mother of my daughters.

The story began out of the water. I was very young, barely 18 years old, and I went to an international swimming competition. Many of my friends were also on that trip, and when we finished the competition, we only wanted one thing: to party!

The next day, the unwanted guest arrived: a nasty hangover. We were in a small town and had to travel to another city. We had bought tickets for the 8:00 AM bus, and obviously we missed it. We couldn't get out of bed. We didn't even make the 10 o'clock, no matter how much we hustled. So, there was no choice but to wait for the 12 o'clock.

The minutes seemed to crawl by, made worse by the sleeplessness and hangover. Athletes like us used to get drunk very easily due to lack of practice. Then, I saw her walking around the station. With all the confidence in the world, I looked at my companions, and told them: "I am going to marry her or someone like her."

I thought she was a beautiful woman, and quite predictably my friends started joking around, saying I was crazy and teasing me until we got on the bus. There she was, and fortunately for me, we were seated in the same row. There was only one empty seat between us.

I looked at my friends and started saying good things about her, while they refuted each one in their eagerness to annoy me. We spoke in Spanish, completely sure that she wouldn't understand. After a long time of analyzing her from head to toe, she turned around, and gently said to us, "When will you stop talking about me?" That's when I found out she was Colombian! We never imagined she spoke Spanish! We all turned pale. And I, who had defended her in all the arguments, mustered up the courage, moved to the seat next to her, and we started talking.

After a few years, remembering that day, Tammy said to me: "I saw you from the moment I arrived at the station, and when I realized that you were going to leave in the same bus, I sat in the back waiting for you to do the same. Then you guys started talking about me, saying things like: "She's a little fat and wears colored contacts, that isn't the real color of her eyes." They kept going until you all looked at me and I said, "I speak Spanish, and yes, this is my eye color. You turned green, remember? I really liked you from the first moment I saw you."

We said goodbye when we arrived at our destination and arranged to meet up that night at an event that would take place in the city's stadium. We almost missed each other! I couldn't get in touch with her, as there were no cell phones and the pay phone was broken, but I didn't know! I spent over 45 minutes trying to dial, but the phone line sounded busy. I could've sworn I would never find her. The stadium was packed, and out of nowhere a tall man with a very thick beard appeared and began to speak to me in a hoarse voice in a language that I did not understand. When he saw my surprised face, he switched to English and said that he was the head of maintenance, that the phone was broken, that he had seen me trying to make a call me for a long time, and he figured it must have been important.

Suddenly, he pulled out a set of keys, opened the pay phone box and connected some wires: "You can make your call now." To this day, I can't figure out how he got there, I believe he was an angel from heaven. If he hadn't shown up, I would never have seen Tammy again. All I had was her phone number, and that night I had to catch a flight to continue my trip. I called, and after several rings, she answered in surprise. She was about to get into the elevator and leave her house. Again, in a matter of seconds, my life changed.

So much had to have happened for me to be with her. That's when I learned to believe in fate! *Que sera, sera. Whatever will be, will be.* We dated long-distance for two years. We communicated by fax and phone, which was very expensive. First, she was in Colombia, then she came to live in Mexico City for college while I was still in Monterrey. We got married when I was 22. Today, I am still convinced that our destiny is to be together.

Over the years we've been married, the stories have multiplied to such an extent that I could write another book or make a movie. One of the most transcendental decisions in the life of a human being is to choose his or her life partner. In our case, we made that decision very young, but without vices, without mixed intentions, with our heart and soul first and foremost. With humility and the desire to learn from each other and become better people by being a couple.

People ask me how it could be that at 22 I made the decision to get married when I was not even in a financial position to make many plans for the future. Simple: it was clear to me that I wanted to spend the rest of my life with her.

Tammy is not only beautiful, she is brilliant in every way. I admire her deeply. Since she appeared in my life, she has helped me put my feet on the ground, to be a better person. My parents taught me how to behave and awakened in me my ambition, in the best sense of the word. She came here to bring me back to Earth. That combination of ambition and humility is what made me dream of being a truly human human being.

Tammy is a woman with many qualities. When we got engaged in 1995, it was clear to me that because of the distance, if she went back to Bogota there would be no shortage of guys willing to take away my opportunity to raise a family with her. It was now or never. And, although our financial situation was not the best, I had already envisioned the best future for both of us, and the first thing to do to achieve it was to be together.

One of the things that most worried Tammy about moving to Monterrey was not being able to travel to Colombia to see her parents. One day, while seeing some friends, someone told her that American Airlines (AA) had a wonderful benefit for its employees: free travel on any flight where there was an empty seat, and if you were married your spouse could fly for free as well, and in first class! That was not all: they offered tickets at ridiculously low prices to other family and friends.

Although Tammy had studied nutrition in college, she found the idea of working for American Airlines to be an incredible solution to the problem of seeing her family more often. She applied for the job, and although she was the only one who had not studied anything related to hospitality and tourism, she got the job. This new job not only solved the problem that was unsettling her, but it changed our lives completely. We were constantly inviting my in-laws up to Monterrey, and we enjoyed several trips together. If under normal conditions my in-laws would have come two or three times a year, with free tickets, they visited six or seven times.

We were very young, and AA gave us a chance to say, "What are we doing this weekend? Do you want to go to Chicago?" In the beginning, we didn't even carry a suitcase because we couldn't afford a hotel, which mattered very little to us because, at that age, comfort takes a back seat. It was just a question of stopping at the airport, checking which flights were available, and getting on a plane that in a couple of hours would have us somewhere screaming from the top of a roller coaster. Afterward, one night in a modest hotel, simple food. In two days, we had taken one of the best trips of our lives.

When things started to get better for us financially, we broadened our horizons. The time came when we could also go to Europe and even stay for a few days. There is nothing better than traveling for free! The American Airlines hub is in Dallas, where we would land without knowing our final destination. We'd get off the plane and run to look at the departure boards: London, Paris, Brussels, Amsterdam, Milan, Rome, Frankfurt, Munich, Madrid. We'd get on whichever flight had seats available. Our favorite place, like so many other people's, was Paris.

We were staying in cheap hotels. The most important thing for me was to be with my favorite person and be happy. What more could we ask for? We would sit in the gardens of the Eiffel Tower park for hours, buy a baguette, pain au chocolat, a bottle of wine, and pass the time watching people walk by, imagining their lives, thinking about ours in the years to come. We had time to talk, to get to know each other, and to fall even more deeply in love. There were no cell phones or any of the technology that exists now. We disconnected from the world and gave each other all the space to listen to each other –it was something spectacular. And so, between trips, we visualized our future.

In my younger days, I learned that the best preparation for achieving something is to visualize it in your mind before it happens. I had been doing this since I was a child, only badly applied because I always visualized catastrophic futures, until I learned to do the little ritual I described previously: getting into a state of deep meditation to 'see' myself swimming the race in the best possible time. Every stroke, every turn, every breath; I literally felt my heart rate rise and my body produce lactic acid. The more I practiced it, the more similar it became to what I saw in my mind and what the stopwatch was telling me, and finally, it was reflected in the time I clocked in each competition. Physical preparation is just as important as mental preparation; the difference between winning and losing is only a few tenths of a second.

I was always a mentally strong person. When I swam well in my mental race, I swam just as well in the real race. The technique worked incredibly for me, so I decided to apply the same philosophy in my marriage, and later, in my business. As my father says, "To build a road, the first thing you have to think about is where it comes from and where it goes." The initial part of my planning is in my mind. First, I visualize it and then I execute it.

Nowadays, when I do a job interview, one of the questions I like to ask a candidate is: "Where do you see yourself in ten years?", and most of the time, the answers are very generic. There is a tendency to respond with abstract answers like "being professionally successful", "living in another country", or "raising a family." When my people address these questions in the recruitment process at Henco, I like the answers to be very personal, that they have enough clarity to say more specific things. People's faces change when you invite them to talk about their deepest dreams, and for me, there is no better way to get to know someone.

Also, talking about your dreams makes the idea stronger within you and outside you. On the one hand, you set goals and commit yourself to them, and on the other hand, you tell the world who you are and what you are looking for. Many will make fun of you, or even call you crazy, but repeating every day what you want to achieve and having the ability to close your eyes and see it, this puts it in your path.

On one of the austere trips we made to Paris, we promised that we would return to this city one day and stay in a beautiful hotel we saw while walking the cobbled streets, which at that time we could not afford. And so, the day would come when we would fulfill our dreams, one by one, step by step. I never spent anything I didn't have, I never got into debt; my mom told me: "First you have to fill your pockets, save. The surplus is the only thing you can spend." Such simple advice saves you from catastrophe when hard times come.

I've always felt like the luckiest man in the world to have found a partner like Tammy, to whom I owe most of what I am now.

They say a man's true success is measured by the size of his wife's smile.

My objective from day one was to make her very happy. I started to listen to her carefully, I was interested in what she wanted, I wanted to be a better person. I learned that when you genuinely care about others, there is a consequence: others will also care about you.

This applies to building the foundation of a marriage and more: relationships with clients, employees, children, co-workers, friends, suppliers, neighbors, and even people you don't know, because caring about the welfare of others makes for a win-win relationship all the time. A smile, a greeting, a word of encouragement can change the day of those who receive it in a positive way, and it costs you absolutely nothing to give it.

For example, if you know your partner likes to spend time with you, give them your time; if you know they like to read, give them the space to do so. If you enjoy exercising, do it together. I remember on one occasion, on vacation in Florence, I had a tremendous craving to eat a Fiorentina steak. Being a huge meat fan, it was the perfect place to indulge. As we were walking to the restaurant, my daughters and wife saw a sign that said: “Vegetarian, vegan, macrobiotic and raw restaurant.” Nothing further from my craving! They were so excited that at that moment I decided to please them, and their gratitude was such that the rest of the trip, they were the ones who wanted to please me. It goes without saying that that same night I ate ‘half a cow’, surrounded by my family’s smiles.

Values come first and then everything else. You have to be ambitious, but humble. Does that sound strange to you? It’s like I’m saying ‘fat’ and ‘thin’ at the same time. Humility is to plant your feet firmly on the ground, no matter the brand of your shoes. One has to be humble to accept reality, without abandoning great aspirations. Ambition must be measured and controlled. Seeking constant growth must be part of every human being’s life, always based on their life purpose. Theodore Roosevelt said it well: “Keep your eyes on the stars and your feet on the ground.”

We have to be aware of our vulnerability, and we as businessmen never want to look vulnerable, even though in reality we are very vulnerable people. Everyone is looking at us and thinking that we have all the answers and that they are the right answers just because we own the business. Nothing could be further from the truth! You must team up with people more talented than you are because, let’s face it: there’s always something you can learn from others. That is why we must listen carefully. We have two ears and one mouth so that we can listen twice as much as we speak.

We too are afraid, we too stop sleeping, we too feel like crying. We are human beings just like everyone else, only we make decisions upon which many people depend. That's why, when we make them, we do so perhaps with courage, even though, inside, we are 'dead scared' and, guess what? It's worth it!

When we've had problems at Henco, I gather the team together and I show my vulnerability. I always open my heart and soul to them, and I tell them the truth. If we work together, we're an insurmountable force and we'll get through it. That's what it's all about –working together, supporting each other. As a team, we have often risen from situations that seem impossible to get out of.

If you're happy about other people's success, you've got it all figured out!

Being grateful, being humble, being afraid, and being vulnerable all lead to a better connection with people. We're human! We all have the same chance to reach for the stars and keep our feet firmly on the ground.

THE MEANING **OF LIFE**

The best moment to believe in
your dreams was when you were a kid.
The second best **moment is today.**

SIMON COHEN
CAP 04

I remember my childhood as a happy time, despite the asthma and my personality weaknesses. Anxiety and fear were already with me, hard to recognize as a child, and I didn't know how to master them. I learned to live with them and control my thoughts. My life has been full of tragedies, 99% of them never happened.

I was an easy child and liked making friends –never problematic, even as a teenager. I guess the 'fear + anxiety' combo made me not even consider breaking the rules. In fact, I have never physically fought with anyone, not even in elementary school. I have always been conciliatory, since I was a child.

I was born in Mexico City in 1974. Although my parents did not come from wealthy families, we never lacked for anything until the first of two major economic crises came along. I don't remember much. It was 1980 and I was about to turn six years old. The dire situation forced us to move to Monterrey, where Rafael, one of my father's brothers lived. He and his family took us into their home for the first few weeks because our financial situation didn't even permit us to rent a place of our own.

Although my mother's family didn't like the idea of us moving to another city, they bid us farewell with a family meal at the home of one of her 11 siblings. That day, my parents, Pepe, and I (Daniel hadn't been born yet), got into our orange 'vochito' (Volkswagen Beetle), with our only worldly belongings, full of hopes and dreams.

Once on the road, I sat looking out the window, pensive. My young mind imagined that the change was for the better. Full of innocence, I asked my parents if we would have a house with a pool and if our school would be bigger and nicer than the one we had gone to in Mexico City. Trying as hard as any parent would be in their situation, they explained to me that things would be 'different', that we would get to live at our uncle's house, and that the school would be much smaller, but that we would have all the necessary conditions to fulfill our dreams living in Monterrey.

After six hours of driving, we stopped in San Luis Potosí. The roads were not like they are now, and it was very tough driving non-stop. It was already very late because the meal at my aunt's house had lasted longer than expected and we had ended up leaving almost at nightfall. The four of us were very tired and our budget for staying in a hotel was limited. My father looked for a room in the cheapest hotels, without success. They told us that the President of Mexico was staying in the city, since he was going to inaugurate a government building the next day. His entourage and companions had filled the hotels to capacity, and there was not much left to choose from. After a couple of hours of twisting and turning, we hadn't found a single available room. I distinctly remember my dad's worried expression. It was almost 3 AM. We couldn't risk taking the road because it was too late and he was already exhausted.

Parked outside a five-star hotel and not knowing what to do anymore, I told my dad: "Let's check it out, what do we have to lose? Don't you worry, I'll use my luck and we'll find something." He smiled. What could a five-year-old do about this problem? When we got out to ask about the rate, we ran into a couple of Presidential

Guards coming out of the hotel. My father approached them and asked if they knew of any nearby, inexpensive place where we could spend the night. He explained that we had been looking for a long time and had not found anything. They turned to look at our car where my mother and my brother Pepe were, and one of them commented: "Our shift starts now, at 3:30, and we have a small room. If you'd like, you can stay there." My dad couldn't believe it. We thanked them and when we told my mom and Pepe what had happened, my dad very solemnly assured them: "We solved it because Simon used his luck." I was very happy.

To this day, recalling this story, when things get complicated and we can't find the way out, my father says to me: "Simon, use your luck." More than 40 years after that incident, and just before he went into the operating room for a very complex surgery, my dad, already on the gurney, looked me in the eyes and repeated this phrase. We couldn't stop the tears. The memories of a lifetime of good and bad memories came to our minds. We had used my luck, which had almost always helped us. This was the most important moment. I would have exchanged all the previous ones to have had luck in this one. We hugged and cried together, hoping for everything to be okay.

One of the qualities we lose when we become adults is the natural energy we have as children. Children, in their innocence, believe in magic all the time, in the unseen and in the adults around them. What they touch emanates that kind of good energy that replicates itself and makes things happen. It seems very important to keep that innocence within us and to be clear that, if we want something to happen, we must first blindly believe that it will happen.

The next morning, still incredulous about what had happened at the hotel, we continued the journey. We got to my aunt and uncle's house, and everything started to take shape. Just as my parents had told me, my new school was very small. There were only six of us in first grade. I was the 'new guy' from another city –skinny, with a thousand allergies and, to top it off, super kind, so... bullying from day one. I learned to defend myself, to earn the respect of my classmates, and it wasn't by fist-fighting them. I thought that if I was kind, quick to forgive, and able to find some way to help, they would just get tired of picking on me. And that's what happened. I was not a pushover at all. It's just that from a very young age, I knew that if you laugh at yourself and make other people's jokes your own, they lose strength and no longer hurt you.

After a time, we were able to rent a modest house a few blocks from school, and I remember playing in an inflatable pool in our small yard 'enjoying' the 100-degree weather of the city. We'd spend hours and hours in that pool. Time flew by. My childhood was a very happy one.

Like any teenager, I had my moments of not understanding my parents and questioning the way we were raised. At 16, you don't even understand yourself, much less those who are giving you the most important lessons of your life. The truth is that once you are an adult or when you become a parent, you understand many things and become very grateful.

Because of issues related to his health, it's emotional for me to talk about my father. I would like to underline how lucky I feel to be part of the family I was born into. The combination of my mother's constant drive and motivation with his teachings of never settling for less: this is the firm ground on which I built my strength and resilience.

My father was the oldest of six brothers. My grandfather was an artist and it was my father who had to financially support the family from the age of 16. He was only able to finish elementary school, because he had to stop studying and find ways to make money and get food on the table. Always tough, always a hard worker. At some point during the 60's and 70's, he traveled around the country selling different products. He's been to many places and has plenty of anecdotes that he enjoys telling. As a food lover, his best stories are always about the dishes he has eaten in every place he visited.

My father was not just a salesman, he was very creative in what he did. He looked for his 'wow factor', the one that makes us different from others and that somehow gives us an advantage over them. For example, at one point in his time as a salesman, fishnet stockings became fashionable, and he was commissioned to sell a large lot in the states on the Mexican Pacific coast. After several days of not having sold anything in the city of Culiacan and already needing to return to Mexico City, he stopped to buy orange juice from a truck that sold the fruits in bulk. The truck driver ended up buying the 4,000 dozen stockings to use as fruit packaging. That's creativity!

These streaks of originality broaden your vision and are likely to lead people to prefer doing business with you rather than with someone else. We all have more than one personal strength that sets us apart, and it is a matter of finding these strengths and using them as tools. The exercise of finding and exploiting them is a fun process and will become your personal or company hallmark.

My father always had a very strong character. He always found a way to be different, to give more, and as we got older, he asked us to do the same. If there was one thing we had at home, it was communication. Imagine, my dad was the first to know when I had my first kiss! Both he and my mother found ways to create spaces to talk with us. We were allowed to argue, with certain sacred exceptions of course, like that time when I was 18, on my way back from a trip, and my father found out that I had gotten a piercing. You don't even want to know. In those times, it was very rare for men to use earrings. Long story short, my new 'bling' spent more time in the ashtray of my car than in my ear. There were things that my father was very firm about: "My way or the highway", or as we say in Spanish, *"Mi casa, mis reglas"* (my house, my rules).

At that age, you don't understand. You argue about everything, and every minute makes you want to question authority at every chance you get. But even in situations like this, in my house I was taught respect and hierarchy. Learning to express and defend my point of view was as important as doing so without offending anyone.

I asked for his opinion all the time. I remember that, when I decided to get married, I asked him if he thought it was a good idea. "This is one of the most important decisions of your life and, in order for you to take responsibility for it and its outcome, you need to make the decision yourself." Such wisdom! If he gave me his opinion and I did well, it would be his merit; if I did badly, it would be his fault. It was a personal decision and that's how I made it.

The same thing happened when I was given the worst grade I had ever received on a math test. Because of my sports commitments, I had been unable to attend classes for several days, and the day I showed up: test! I didn't know anything, I was not even close to solving a single problem. When I got my grade, I was fine with my 2 out of 10. The problem was how I'd tell my dad. I approached him and asked him to have one of the private talks we regularly had. With a firm and convincing voice, I said, "Daddy, I've decided I want to be a doctor, a surgeon." He was surprised. I never liked needles, and seeing blood made me faint. My father knew that one of my biggest challenges was dealing with numbers; math and I have always had a complicated relationship. Then he asked me why my decision was so sudden, to which I replied: "It's one of the professions that doesn't involve math." And then I showed him my terrible grade. He laughed, but he never said no to me. He knew there was something behind the news I tried to sell him, and my cunning could never beat his experience. He knew me too well.

He has always been a demanding father, but he let us live our lives, make decisions, and therefore learn that there are consequences we had to live with. "Every action has a consequence, so before you do anything, think about the future", he'd say.

Acknowledgments and expressions of gratitude to parents must be made while they're still alive. I always tried to be very open about my feelings, and the climax was in January 2020. For two years, we were fortunate enough to have Harvard University work on a case study on Henco and our High Performance, Happy People culture. They liked it so much that they even made a documentary. I couldn't be more proud of this! Our 'small big company' would be, from that day on, an example of how to treat its employees, customers, and suppliers in a very humane way. The happiness and good vibes we decided to achieve at Henco were transcending.

The day of our first appearance at Harvard I decided to invite my parents and my brothers. Tammy and the most senior company directors would go to the second and third day of events. It was the perfect moment to thank my parents and brothers, and to pay tribute to them while still alive. Imagine my parents' marvel, having only studied through the sixth grade, to know that on this day, their child was going to be applauded at the best university in the world. I wanted the spotlight to be on them: "The more I praise my people, the more I praise myself", I thought.

Nights before, I thought about what I would say in front of the teachers and businessmen who were studying our case. I visualized myself once, I visualized myself a hundred times. I was **FULFILLED** and I wanted to pass this feeling on to my special guests. The center of attention should be my family, not me, not the achievements that Henco had, but how they, along with Tammy and my daughters, inspired me to always give my best.

My speech was not about Henco or Simon Cohen, but about a family that had lived through some crises, about parents who had pulled us through every moment, giving us everything even when we had nothing. It was a story of struggle that had all of us as main characters and me as a man extremely grateful and lucky to be one of them. When I mentioned that they were with me in the room that day, the audience began to applaud. My family got up from their seats and people clapped even louder, giving them a standing ovation for a couple of minutes. Gone were the differences, the moments of tension, and estrangement.

I looked at my parents from the stage and felt that I could finally give back at least a little of what they had given me. The energy I felt in the room was indescribable, and practically everyone in the audience had tears in their eyes. The applause echoed in my soul, and I knew the same thing happened to my parents, because when we left, my dad told me something that I will carry in my heart all my life: "Simon, you are my idol. The only thing I can feel right now is ecstasy –there is nothing more to say", and he hugged me tight.

That same day, I met with a second group of business-men, and later there would be a lunch in our honor. In the classroom, there was another standing ovation. Once again, I got goosebumps and cried because of the energy and the emotions in the room. I seized the opportunity to thank my parents for something different. In the Q&A session, one of the attendees asked my parents to give them the recipe of how they had raised such a united family. My father said, "With unconditional love", and he began to cry with emotion.

Before the lunch, my parents had stepped out for coffee and arrived a few minutes after I had started my speech. When they entered the dining room, the group of businessmen noticed their presence –it was the loudest applause of the day. Seven standing ovations at Harvard University in one day is not an easy thing to achieve. I'm very proud to have paid that homage to my parents while they're still with us.

Don't wait until your loved ones are gone to miss them and thank them; if you are one of the lucky ones who still has them with you, call them right now and tell them how much you love them!

No matter how, as long as they are with you, even for one day, because that's the law of life: you eventually will not be able to do so. Don't let pride take that privilege away from you.

Our adrenaline levels were very high, and we were wearing our hearts on our sleeves. When we finished, the five of us sat together in a private room and talked about how unreal this moment seemed, how lucky we were. My brothers said something that left a mark on us all: "This moment is unique. It is something magical and it probably won't happen again." My father sat on a long sofa. Because of his poor health, he looked very tired, but with a smile that I had never seen before. He beckoned to us, asked us to get close to him, and started crying. The five of us hugged for a long time and thanked each other. Each and every one of us had done our part to achieve this dream. The applause had been our public homage; this embrace was our family homage.

There is no such thing as the perfect family. There is the family you have, and unconditional love is what makes it special for everyone. In my opinion, there is nothing more important than being united. Sometimes we fight with a brother or a father over nonsense. It's not worth it! Think about it and forgive. To forgive is not to forget; to forgive is to remember things without anger.

I know that there will be new disagreements, that being a happy family –as I have already said– is also about accepting everyone's imperfection with humility, remaining empathetic, and always looking out for each other. It is knowing how to give, and the only thing you can get in return are blessings.

ooo

My mother comes from a very large and conservative family, so her life as a student ended in the sixth grade. Her parents believed that women did not have to keep going to school after a certain grade. My mother married at 22, a little 'late' compared to the average age women in her family got married.

The clearest example of the beliefs that my mother's family had is that my grandparents, her parents, were engaged when my grandfather was seven and my grandmother was two. Unbelievable! They were born in

Aleppo, Syria, and because of the war and the fact that they were Jewish, they had to flee. They took a boat to France, and from there they embarked with the intention of reaching New York, where my grandfather's brother lived. At the first stop, not speaking English and only a little French, my grandfather asked if they had reached their destination, the captain's answer was yes, and they disembarked. While searching for the Statue of Liberty, they came across Café de la Parroquia. They had disembarked in Veracruz! Without speaking the language, without contacts, and without money, they had to earn their living by working hard and being very creative. A few years later, they went to live in Mexico City, where they got married when my grandmother was just 14 and my grandfather 19.

My mother married very much in love and with many dreams. When we arrived in Monterrey in 1980, my father and his brother Rafael, supported by my mother, started a textile business. She learned design, and at the same time took care of her three children. Conversations in my house went on forever because of company matters, and she didn't hesitate to make her point. When we went through critical moments, she stood firm and with every action, however minimal, she made it clear that everything she did was for her husband and children.

She's had to blaze a trail throughout her life. Being the ninth of 11 siblings, in order to be heard she had to attract attention and express her feelings. She instilled this in us. In addition to being an extremely present mom, she took it upon herself to nurture our inner strength. In my case, so sickly as a child, so afraid of many things, she would say to me: "You can do it, don't be intimidated" and "Show them who you are, you are no less than anyone else." She is an excellent motivator and to this day, she insists that we be disciplined and go in the right direction.

My 'Warrior Woman', as we called her in the video we made for her 60th birthday, is the most caring person in the world. Before thinking about herself, she has made sure that the rest of us are not hungry, cold, or thirsty. In her family, gift-giving was not considered important, but far from not knowing how to give, she is someone who gives herself completely and with her hands and arms full. To her grandchildren, for example, she gives as many gifts as they are years old: five years old, five gifts; ten years old, ten gifts. It is her greatest joy! Each of the gifts is thoughtful and planned so as to make them smile. That's my mother.

This is a very important lesson. I believe that many people use their life stories to justify their faults. In my mother's case, she decided to turn shortcomings into reasons to give, and to try to make those around her as happy as possible. This is something I emphasize to my daughters: learn from the good and learn from the bad in your parents. We are not perfect beings, and there's nothing better than for our daughters –in learning from our mistakes– to seek to be an improved version of ourselves. The aim of parenting should not be to create people in your own image, but to make each generation aware of the good and the bad in order to improve on the previous one.

Since we first arrived in Monterrey, one of my mom's biggest frustrations was that, even though she came from a very large family, we would grow up far away from our grandparents, uncles, and cousins. This led her to be very persistent, almost obsessive, in making us a united family. Her tireless work and unconditional love have achieved it: family meals every Wednesday and dinner on Friday, and no one wants to miss them. We created an open and joyful atmosphere with a lot of communication, sharing this time with brothers, in-laws, and cousins. Much of the strength my brothers and I have to continue working together was inspired by my mother.

My mother is a direct and transparent woman, and she has the biggest heart in this world. Today, she devotes her time to helping those who need it most, and she goes out of her way to help people she doesn't even know. She always means well and thinks of others before herself. As Gandhi said, "The best way to find yourself is to lose yourself in the service of others."

ooo

Each family is different, and in our traditions, we have customs based on family unity as the nucleus of society. In the case of 'these Cohens', I'd say we've always been quite close.

Anyone who has two brothers knows that the first-born gets the toughest rules, the middle child is still a trial run, and the little one –who gets the most seasoned parents– gets much looser limits. In our case, Pepe, the eldest, paved the way for me to arrive two years later, and eight years after me, Daniel.

You'd think that all siblings would have to be very similar because they grew up in the same house and have the same parents. As it turns out, that is not the case: the three Cohens have very different personalities. However, when it comes to team building, we complement each other. The strengths of one are the weaknesses of the other, and vice versa. As in any good soccer team, you need goalkeepers, defense, midfielders, and strikers. Our differences have made us strong.

When two people think alike, one of them is redundant.

After all the trials we have been through together, I am convinced that my brothers are my heroes in flesh and blood.

At a time when our relationship was strained by business issues, arguments with them represented a sad and wearisome activity. My immaturity and lack of experience led me to see only one side of things: my own. When you cling to the idea that your vision is the only right one, the consequence is that perspective is limited and, therefore, you automatically close many doors that can lead you to a better result. Empathy is being able to see for a moment with your own eyes what others are feeling; it is the possibility of sitting in the other's chair and trying to understand their vision, to find points of agreement, and to start building from there.

These episodes of family crisis provide enormous opportunities for enlightenment. They teach us how to listen to others, how to yield, and how to concede. When we think of the word 'negotiate', we usually relate it to business issues, but the truth is that personal relationships that grow and last are based on this: on knowing how to negotiate all the time.

One of the things that most marked me when I returned from China and saw my brothers again was something that Pepe said to me with a broken soul and tears in his eyes: "You got sick because of us." I was touched by my brother's big heart and humility, acknowledging that the situation had led us all to unnecessary wear and tear! It was a wake-up call for all four of us. Pepe didn't mean that they had connected an extra wire to my heart to send me electric shocks. He knew that the frictions of family negotiation had caused too much stress on me, precisely because of the love we have for each other. When I remember the arguments, it is clear to me that beyond the heat of the moment and the anger, what we really felt was a deep sadness and an enormous frustration in realizing that we were not succeeding in reaching a positive conclusion. We all felt the same way, but our pride wouldn't let get there.

From then on, the bond with my brothers went through a gradual transformation that, to this day, makes me appreciate those complicated times as tests that we overcame as a team. Together we have built not only a solid Henco based on shared values, but other companies in different industries that today are examples of humanism and productivity. High Performance, Happy People is present in everything we do. If we hadn't learned in time to understand each other and respect each other, I don't know where we would be today. Respect is a required value for any relationship, and the definition I like best is: "Respect is the right of others to think differently than you."

Pepe, as a good big brother, has been my example to follow. I can describe him in two words: loyal and generous. His values come before all else. It is true that feisty discussions can always be had with him, as true as it is that his heart is the biggest in the world, and that at his center, what matters most to him is having a united family. Listening to him speak is a constant lesson for me. He has clarity, and if it is his turn to take you on, he will do so with sound arguments.

Daniel, on the other hand, is the analyst. His thinking is mathematical, and I, who have always been at odds with numbers, admire his precision and intelligence. My younger brother 'is always Switzerland' in any situation. He doesn't like to fight and has impressive lucidity. In terms of charisma and sociability, Daniel has them in spades. He is the kind of person who, when he sets his mind to something, there is no human power that can stop him.

It fills me with peace to look at my daughters as there are also three of them and with such different personalities. If I take our example, I know that they will always have each other, no matter what. I know that having siblings is a blessing because there is no friend more unconditional than the one with whom you share blood and the first memories of life.

From the moment we found out that Tammy was pregnant with our first child, I felt an enormous thrill. I was going to be a dad, and it was going to be a girl. Of course, I never imagined it would be not just one, but three girls in all. They arrived and transformed our entire world, and out of all the dreams I have fulfilled with my wife, they are, without a doubt, the best.

When they were very young, I believed that being a father meant being a good provider. After China and after the trip to the beach, I understood that we had a huge responsibility to teach these three human beings, and that to achieve this, all three needed all the time and love that we could give them. When we founded Henco, I was the kind of busy parent who thought the few hours I gave my daughters were 'quality time'. Time is time, and we cannot replace it with 15-minute hours, no matter how hard we try. Then we seek to give them 'a toy' to ease our conscience. Let's stop buying our children what we never had and start teaching them everything we learned. The essential is invisible.

There is no point in overwhelming them with gifts if we do not nurture their spirits. It's not about believing that your children are an extension of you, but about giving them the tools to face life as it is, to make their own mistakes, and have the strength to take responsibility for themselves. My daughters will tell you I'm not a nagging dad. And I don't mean to say that when I promised them that I would be a happy man, I would be smiling all day long. A happy person obviously has the right to be angry or sad!

It's okay to NOT be okay; it's part of being human.

This philosophy of happiness helps you get out of any negative situation much faster because you understand and really think that everything happens for a reason, and that everything is for the best.

I'm not the perfect dad, and I don't want to have perfect daughters. What I am describing is just my experience and my point of view on things. We can't deny that we have been wrong, both them and us as parents, but in our relationship, love and the desire to continue growing are what prevail.

I try to almost never scold them. Instead of giving them a sermon, I would rather explain things and be sure that they trust us enough to tell us everything. If there is good news, I will certainly celebrate with them, and if not, I will be there to remind them that they can learn a lesson from what happened. Of course, there are no recipes for being a parent, and, of course, one can be filled with phrases and advice. But today more than ever, I believe that the best way to educate is first, to be willing to make mistakes and second, to teach by example.

My daughters are young today and none of the three remember clearly what happened to me in 2006. Which means that, if I had not made it, not one of them would remember me. I would have missed everything for nothing. Life gave me a second chance just in time.

FULFILLED

LIFE IS NOT **A REHEARSAL**

Do what is difficult and your life will be easy; do what is easy and your life will be difficult.

Who is Simon? I would say that I am a dreamer, a person who is passionate about life, someone who understood that his purpose in life is to spread happiness. I enjoy every moment, every minute of the day. I like to be with my friends –I consider myself a very social person– and to learn: I am an avid learner! You can't teach if you're not willing to learn and do so constantly.

The future belongs to those who learn, unlearn, and relearn.

If you don't say, "I behaved so foolishly a year ago", you didn't learn enough this year.

Besides, I love to work, I love what I do, and I put a lot of passion into it. A lot of people think: "Sure, you're the happiest person in the world because your company is successful", and my answer is: "No, sir, it's the other way around, our company is successful because we decided to be happy and work on this every day." Success is a consequence of being happy.

Happiness is not something random. It is not a treasure found at the end of the rainbow like the pot of gold in fairy tales. Happiness involves working and valuing what has been achieved, whether it's big or small, a lot or a little. If you're not happy with everything you have, you won't be happy with everything you lack either. We need to learn to want what we have and not have what we want. That will give us stable and prolonged happiness. And for all this to become a reality, discipline is necessary.

To be happy implies a complete change of habits, and we know that this is not achieved overnight. For there to be a transformation, there needs to be change in more than one area of your life. Changing habits requires a radical and integral transformation.

By imposing a certain internal discipline, we can experience a transformation in our attitude, perspective, and approach to life. In general terms, one begins by identifying the factors that lead to happiness and those that lead to suffering. Once that is done, it is necessary to gradually eliminate those that lead to suffering by cultivating those that lead to happiness.

When I decided to be a **FULFILLED** man, I made a commitment, first to myself and then to the people around me. Not only did I decide to be happy, I also wanted to multiply my happiness and spread it to others. I was more convinced than ever that for my plans to be truly great, I had to influence more people. And I discovered something that may sound contradictory to what I've said so far: being happy also means having the patience and self-esteem to accept that not every day will be a happy day.

What I set out to do was to make a complete change in my worldview. I wasn't looking to join the 'optimist club' and smile even when I felt like crying. What I envisioned –and this is my way of thinking to this day– is that everything happens for a good reason, although many times we may not understand that reason in the moment. Time needs to pass in order for us to discover the treasure that life has given us.

And how do we discover that treasure? In my experience, there are six basic values that help you find it more easily:

- Gratitude
- Trust
- Respect
- Integrity
- Humility
- Attitude

When I started delegating, given no other choice by the circumstances, I understood that there were people better than me, and that as a team we would be stronger. The true trial by fire for any entrepreneur is when he decides to become a businessman and let go of control. In my experience, it was a really difficult process because I had a hard time delegating. It's like letting your child go, telling them they have to leave home, and trusting them to do better than you did. There are things we can control and things we cannot, so why beat ourselves up about it? Let's work on what is within our reach, and what's not, let's toss it up!

Let's control what we can, and what we can't, let the universe fix it.

Only in this way will we be able to enjoy the little things that make up life and lead you to fulfillment. For an entrepreneur to let go is to learn to delegate, to put controls in place, to establish a well-configured Board of Directors, to trust people, and have them trust you.

It is not easy. For your team to come in and tell you that you're wrong, to have the humility to bow your head and acknowledge that it's true –it is not easy. I used to be omnipotent. In my office, I did whatever I wanted. When you institutionalize a business, when you want to take it to the next level, it is crucial to be aware of the step you are taking, from being an entrepreneur to becoming a businessman.

If you want to be a good businessman, you need to surround yourself with people who are better than you, and then allow them to fly. That's just what happened with Manuel, a friend since college. Back in school, we had said, "Someday we'll work together."

Aside from being an exceptional person, Manuel was always excellent with books. We complemented each other because I'd always been good with people. Manuel is very intelligent. Over the years, he began to evolve in his career as a high-level executive and he did very well. When I decided to move to Mexico City, I called him and invited him to lunch to tell him it was time to work together. Manuel was working in a multinational company, and the way to test if we could work as a team was to hire him to do a consulting project outside of working hours. I needed him to design a control panel to remotely check the company's productivity indicators. For the next two months, he came to my office every afternoon not knowing that I had a secret plan: I wanted to see how he worked and if he fit in with the company's organizational culture.

Setting up the control panel involved talking to each of the directors and interacting with them. Afterwards,

I went around asking for my directors' opinions about Manuel's performance. They agreed: he's a very bright guy, he 'knows his stuff', he's very tidy, he's very cool. One of them, Héctor, already knew him because they went to school together as kids.

Manuel went through all the departments, and one day he said, "The project is ready." He showed me the control panel. "Do you like it?" he asked me. After a few minutes of admiring the outcome and analyzing it in depth, I replied: "I love it, but you have to like it, not me. I would like you to work at Henco and implement it yourself." That's how I invited him to be part of the company, not without first discussing it with my partners and my team, and knowing that we agreed that he was the right person for the job.

Manuel set only one condition to accept my proposal: that I slowly let him operate independently, that I trust him and his work, because without that, he could not give me his best. As Warren Buffett says, "You can hire good people and let them work, or you can hire cheap people and tell them what they have to do."

He joined in 2011 as Vice President. Today, Manuel is Henco's CEO. Why? Because, in that regard, he's more capable than I am, more organized. He's what the company needed. What brought us to where we are will not take us to where we dream of going. That's why I had to make decisions and evolve.

With that humility, with our feet on the ground, we both understood each other and, without rushing, we took the big step. With Manuel as CEO, I was able to move with my wife and daughters to Mexico City. We had been thinking about it for several years. We made the change thanks to the support of my team, and I will never stop thanking them.

ooo

Gratitude is one of the values I hold dearest. It is the purest feeling a human being can have. If you're not grateful, problems will come your way in droves. If you are, you'll always have solutions within your reach.

Complaining brings scarcity, gratitude brings abundance.

You must thank your parents, your friends, your siblings, your teachers, the people who have taught you valuable lessons. I am convinced that in order to be successful, and above all to be happy, gratitude is key. Besides, when you say thank you, it's like an automatic reaction and it changes your life. If you approach someone, smile at them, and thank them, you can really change their life. It's a fundamental feeling we need. There's nothing more essential.

I am grateful even to the people who hurt me for the lessons they taught me. Sometimes people turn against you, and that helps you grow towards being a better person. If we understand it that way, it's a great way to help yourself. This is one quality of very mature people.

ooo

Another key element is trust. If you lose it or if you feel threatened, you will raise a barrier that will not let you be free. Trust is not something that is given halfway. It is or it isn't, it's black or white, with no middle ground. Earning other people's trust is not easy and requires a lot of focus. Failure to do so can be a turning point in your professional life. Getting it right can catapult you to another level. And that's how it happened to me.

In 2000, just as I was taking off as an entrepreneur, I decided to visit one of the most important multinationals and offer them my services. Nobody knew me then. Cold call. "Miss, my name is Simon Cohen and I'd like an appointment with the Logistics Director." After several attempts, the day was finally here! Like every other day, and regardless of the 110-degree weather that is summer in Monterrey, I put on my suit and tie and headed to this company hopeful and with a hunger for triumph. My appointment was at 11. I got there on time.

I announced myself at the reception desk and the lady kindly asked me to wait. Minutes passed, hours passed, and no one came to greet me. At 3 PM, after four hours of waiting, I was told that the person who was going to meet with me was very busy, and if I could please return the next day at the same time.

I repeated my ritual the next morning and headed to the meeting once again. Again on time, I greeted the lady with a wide smile. She asked me to wait again. Officially embarrassed, and after another four hours of waiting, she asked me to come back the next day. I can't deny that it made me very angry. However, I also imagined that if this gentleman was a normal guy, he would feel a little bit guilty and this would be an advantage for me in my attempt to become his supplier.

On the third day, I showed up just like the two previous days, smiling, a bit uncertain about what had happened, but without losing hope. At 11 AM, they sent me in. The person who welcomed me, very experienced and with a serious countenance, listened attentively. “You have a lot to offer”, he said. “You’re a very persistent person and you deserve a chance.” I couldn’t get over my excitement when I left the meeting. The first thing I did was call all the people who had told me to give up and tell them about my great achievement.

Since then, I promised myself to put in my best effort to offer them a service superior to anything they had ever received. I’d be looking out for them 24/7. I knew my competition wouldn’t do that and this was my competitive advantage. Once inside as a supplier, nothing and no one would push me out.

The first shipments were successful. The containers came and went properly and on time. The level of customer satisfaction was increasing every day, and the business relationship was constantly growing, to the point that sales to this multinational represented more than 50% of my company’s sales. “This is not healthy”, I thought, “I have to get two or three more clients like this.”

The search began and the results started showing, except that the level of service I had been used to giving to this client demanded a lot of my time. Until one day, the unexpected happened.

It was in the days leading up to the 2006 World Cup in Germany, and this company had put out a very important campaign for its consumers. Prizes would be given in stamps that come inside their packaging. World Cup trips, promotional items, televisions, etc. My contact called me and asked me to pick up the product in China. We immediately contacted the supplier, and had everything ready for departure. 48 hours before collection, we were informed that the product did not pass quality control tests and had been rejected in its entirety, impossible to use! We immediately informed the client, who contacted the supplier. After much negotiation, they found an alternate supplier, this time in Buenos Aires, Argentina.

Due to the quality issue delay, and with time running out with the start of the World Cup campaign, we were asked to fly the merchandise in. "I need it to arrive before Friday, otherwise the product will be completely damaged, and we won't be able to start the campaign", he said. "This would bring lawsuits from consumers and that's something we cannot allow. We already announced this on TV, in the press, and on the radio. You cannot let me down."

I checked with my team and we opted to pay the airline the premium rate. Ezeiza (Buenos Aires), Viracopos (Sao Paulo), Memphis (United States), Mexico City. This was the route.

On Monday at 9 PM, we collected the product without a hitch. We went through Customs in Buenos Aires, and the flight took off punctually at 3 AM on Tuesday. The moment I heard the plane had taken off,

I informed the client. I couldn't sleep while waiting for the connection in Sao Paulo. When they announced the departure of the flight from Sao Paulo to Memphis, I took a deep breath and thought we were very close to achieving our goal of delivering on time. An accident on the plane during take-off crushed my excitement. I turned pale. The plane had gone off the runway, and the delivery was now at risk. We had to be very creative and use all our connections to accomplish the 'miracle' of delivering the cargo before Friday in Mexico City.

We moved heaven and earth, managed to get the cargo out of the crashed plane, and checked it in on a commercial flight from an alternate airport to Mexico City. We invested a significant amount of resources to accomplish this, without asking the client if they were going to pay us for the additional expense. It didn't matter: we were responsible for delivering on time, although not for the accident, these things can happen in logistics. We couldn't fail them or lose our main client's trust.

On Thursday at around midnight, the plane miraculously took off with the entire, undamaged product shipment, directly from Sao Paulo to Mexico City and scheduled to land at 8 AM. I finally slept. The plane landed on time, and after the unloading maneuvers, the next step was Customs. At that point, they told me that the system was down and that they wouldn't be able to process anything until Monday!

None of these events depended on me, nor were they something I could control. I poured myself into this one hundred percent, and even then, we would not be able to avoid the apparent economic tragedy that our client would endure. I was devastated. I got a call from the company's Logistics Director, who was furious and incapable of listening reasonably. He threatened me. He told me that all the lawsuits would be directed at us and we would surely go bankrupt. Exhausted and disappointed, but calm because we had done our best, I shed tears of anger and went home.

On Monday afternoon, I received a call from our client, asking to meet the next day with the CEO. I was shaking. I didn't know what was going to happen or what trouble I could possibly get into. I arrived on time on Tuesday, and they ushered me into his office. I had never seen such a big and fancy office. I sat down and was asked for a detailed explanation of the facts. I finished telling the story thoroughly, and after a brief silence, the CEO replied: "This is the kind of company we have to work with. Regardless of the result, they gave more than one hundred percent of themselves and invested without expecting anything in return, solely in the pursuit of fulfilling agreements. Starting today, I want you to be our long-term strategic ally. Please, start reviewing the contracts."

There is no doubt that the lesson learned is that you must always give yourself to the maximum, despite being in the most adverse of circumstances. Trust is either earned or lost. This time, it was our turn to win. Like the song says:

Sometimes you win by losing and there's no way to fail if you give it your all.

To this day, this multinational is one of our main strategic allies. Every time we tell this story, we share a smile of satisfaction.

ooo

Respect is another crucial element and, as I have said, it means recognizing other people's right to think differently than you do. At Henco, we love to listen. Everyone's voices are worth the same and we give each voice the value it deserves. Leaders who don't listen will eventually be surrounded by people who have nothing to say. We love to question. As Confucius said: "The person who asks may look foolish for a minute; the person who does not ask will be foolish all his life."

Although this company is very fun and we openly laugh at ourselves, we do it within a friendly atmosphere and without wishing to offend anyone. You are never too important to not be nice to people. This was understood from the first day we started the High Performance, Happy People culture. Today, people of different religions or creeds, nationalities, races, ages, sexual preferences, and physical conditions work at Henco. They are loved and respected equally.

One time while traveling in Canada, we met with Prime Minister Justin Trudeau. After greeting him excitedly, I asked him what he thought was the secret of success. He answered firmly: "Diversity is our strength." And there can be no diversity without respect.

ooo

The fourth element is **integrity.** What is it? Simple: integrity is doing the right thing even when no one is watching. It's that hard and that easy. When you live in such a complicated society, used to doing things in an improvised manner, someone with integrity encounters many obstacles.

What is right is right even if no one does it, and what is wrong is wrong even if everyone does it.

We're as straight arrow as can be at Henco. As a society, we lack integrity. Life would be so much easier if more people had integrity. When I started in this business, someone told me, "You're walking into an industry of pirates." Still in college, I visited a forwarding company –the industry I belong to– and I got to see how the owner gave a wad of bills to another company's buyer to ensure his shipments.

Why did he have to give him money? If he does his job well, provides high-quality service, and charges a fair price? It really angered me. It was as if the one who received the money was not happy with the service and the one who gave it stopped working because he had the other guy bought. It created a huge conflict for me.

I thought: "I don't want my company to ever have to give a single peso to do business."

Since then and to this day, in our company we have a zero-tolerance policy towards corruption. When you witness an act like that, so vile, it's an invitation to do the right thing. If there were more people wanting to act correctly, we would be closer to living in peace and finding happiness.

I started working in this industry in the late 90's, and about 80% of the operations were carried out with bribes. From the beginning at Henco, we acted with integrity and proved to ourselves that things can be done the right way. If someone asks for a 'commission' on shipments, they are not given anything, it's that simple. Integrity is a value at this company, a pillar of our culture.

People frequently ask me what the difference is between integrity and honesty. I recently heard a story about a couple who were in a hotel and ordered pizza. When they got their pizza, they noticed that there was an envelope inside the box, and when they opened it, they found a thousand dollars. She got all excited, "Let's go shopping!" While the man judiciously took the envelope and said, "This money is not ours." He got dressed and went to the pizzeria. When he arrived, he asked for the manager, who, seeing the envelope and with tears in her eyes said: "I have saved all year to buy my children's Christmas presents. My hiding place was the pizza box behind my desk. Today we sold so much that someone took the box and it ended up with you. You are an angel."

What an honest guy, but the story's not over... To show her appreciation, the manager suggested they take a picture to upload to social media to tell the world that there were still honest people out there. Surprised, our main man exclaimed: "No way, don't even think about taking my picture." "Why?" asked the manager. "Because the woman I'm with at the hotel is not my wife."

This is precisely the difference between honesty and integrity. Honesty is about your outwards actions: what I do, what I say, my public actions. Integrity is doing the right thing even when no one is watching: who I am, what I think, and my private actions.

ooo

I firmly believe that humility is one of the most important characteristics a good leader should have. Dream big with your feet firmly on the ground. It sounds difficult to be ambitious and humble at the same time. How do you combine them? Ambition is focused on the collective, on the company's growth towards a common goal. Humility is found within the individual.

Your example as a leader should inspire others to be humble, while you continue to be the leader of a team with big goals and ambition.

In other words, if there are ten of us, humble, hard-working people who accept our flaws and virtues, and together we dream something big, we will for sure obtain it. It's not just about aspiring to greatness, but also about feeding our ambition to keep growing. Greatness with humility and with ambition.

A mistake that makes you humble is much more valuable than an achievement that makes you arrogant.

Manuel's first year at Henco was a transitional period. Little by little, he took over responsibilities, making decisions, and earning people's respect. We worked side by side and we consulted with each other on everything. We started dividing tasks and learning from one another. He from my passion for sales and desire to grow, and I from his organization and capacity for analysis.

In 2012, our agent in France invited us to a global convention in Paris. When I looked at the dates, it was a packed schedule, with only 48 hours to get there and back, it was crazy! I got together with Manuel, who was Vice President, Héctor our Operations Director, and Christopher Pérez our Purchasing Director, and we decided that the four of us would go together and divide the work. One would deal with all the issues related to Asia, another with Europe, another with administrative issues, and I would do the long-term strategy with the management team. We were ready for one more adventure.

When we wrapped up the planning, Héctor came up to me and thanked me for the opportunity to travel to Europe. "This is the first time I'm going across the pond", he said. Excited, I went home with a task: how could I give greater recognition and show appreciation to the people who had given me so much? The next morning, I called them again to a meeting in my office, and excitedly said: "I have good news for you guys. Since I consider traveling the best experience you can have, and I want to share it with you, I would like you to invite your wives on this trip. Here are the tickets for you to go on a two-week, all-expenses-paid vacation together to tour the Old Continent."

Nothing gives me more joy than giving. Even though I knew they would miss work time, the human side has always been a priority for me. It's the best investment. They left a week before the convention, and when we met in Paris, I had the opportunity to spend time with them and their wives, all wonderful people. We hadn't taken the time to get to know each other before, and we had an incredible time, roaring with laughter! To the point that waiters in restaurants we would come and congratulate us on the great vibe we had. Being together enjoying a good meal and a glass of wine was enough to be **FULFILLED!**

We did very well at the convention, and as soon as it was over, I went back to Mexico. A few weeks later, Manuel came to my office and very excitedly said: "I have only been at Henco for a year and a few months, but it will be engraved in my heart for life. We are going to have a baby 'made in France'! The stork is going to bring it to us from Paris." We laughed and gave each other a big hug. Now Henco had left its mark on their lives forever.

It was not the first nor the only time we had done this kind of thing at Henco. There is no doubt that it is a way of life, and I too have been moved to tears by tremendous surprises. In 2017, I was awarded the title of "The Most Trusted CEO in Mexico" by Great Place to Work Institute. For me, this represented an enormous responsibility, since it was Henco's own employees and other Mexican businessmen who voted for me to be given this great honor.

This compels me to continue with high-quality performance, to dream big, to have very ambitious goals, and to give it my all together with my team, and the necessary humility to listen, correct, change course, accept my mistakes, and bow my head. Being happy and working with integrity were two vital factors in receiving this acknowledgment –how I would like to see a world full of happy, whole people! Now it turns out that my wanting to be happy and to spread this happiness was deserving of a prize for which I am deeply grateful, but shouldn't this be what's normal?

"Nothing in nature lives for itself. The rivers do not drink their own water; the trees do not eat their own fruit; the sun does not shine on itself and flowers do not spread their fragrance for themselves. Living for others is a rule of nature. We are all born to help each other. No matter how difficult it is...Life is good when you are happy; but much better when others are happy because of you", as Pope Francis said.

ooo

There is one thing that is yours, only yours, and yours alone: your attitude. Victor Frankl said, "Everything can be taken from a man but one thing: the last of the human freedoms—to choose one's attitude in any given set of circumstances, to choose one's own way." I understand that we're not perfect, that we are human and make mistakes, and there are very difficult situations that are beyond our control. As in logistics, if a ship sinks, it's not on me, nor if a container is stolen. What does depend on me is the attitude with which I take on the situation, solving it opportunely, closing the chapter, and carrying on.

This applies to your personal life, too. When you have a problem, don't dwell on it; solve it and move on. Small problems, simple solutions; face it and break it down before the problem grows and puts an end to you and your energy.

We all have problems. There is not a person on the planet who doesn't have them. We came to this planet to solve them. That's how it is. There are those who have many, those who have less, and there are only two ways to face them: angry and with negative energy, or with positive energy, thinking that everything is for the better. It depends on you! There is no such thing as an obstacle-free path. Once, a person who had a serious accident was asked, "How can you be so positive after losing your legs?" He replied, "How can you be so negative when you have both of yours?" That is having a positive attitude!

I'm one of those people who love and admire their in-laws very much. 'Don Nemo', as he is called, is a great human being, intelligent and practical, with an absurdly contagious philosophy of life. My mother-in-law, 'Doña Alice', left us too soon, just a few months ago, leaving a deep hole in my heart. A noble person, a lover of books and art, we admired each other in a special way. The day she went away, I felt like I lost my number-one fan.

Once, my in-laws came up from Colombia to visit us in Monterrey. I had been working on a project for six months to get some huge transformers to repair. The logistical issue was very complicated –shallow water, excessively heavy and oversized, a genuine nightmare– and I asked for help from experts in order to win the tender.

The day before the publication of the tender, I received a call telling me that we were the imminent winners. I can't tell you how excited I was! I sought out some of these experts and shared my joy with them. One of them went behind my back and called our supplier; together, they put in a bid with a proposal 1% cheaper than mine. The project to which I had devoted so much time had been snatched away from us.

I was beyond furious, rage invading my whole body, tingling from head to toe. I got home, bristling, and there was 'Don Nemo', as level-headed as ever. I told him what had happened, and in his eagerness to reassure me, he said, "Don't worry, everything in this life is for the best." I couldn't believe what he was saying to me. How could a person think that there was anything positive in losing a project that big, after having dedicated such an enormous effort towards winning it? I excused myself, went to my room, and shut the door behind me.

Months later, I received another call that made me understand what my father-in-law had said. I was told that the machinery moved by the supplier and the person who undercut us (the same ones I would have used to execute the project) had had an accident. They were both in serious trouble for not paying attention to certain small details. Had I won the tender initially, I would probably have been the one affected, and Henco would have been caught in a very serious situation! Everything happens for a reason, for something good, although sometimes we cannot understand it at that moment.

Remember that from time to time, not getting what you want is a tremendous stroke of luck!

The attitude we decide on having when faced with life's obstacles, successes, or failures, depends on us. Let's always see the glass as half full!

"You can't connect the dots by looking forward; you can only do it by looking backward. So, you have to trust that they will connect positively in some way in the future."

I had worked on this project all by myself, without any help. It was exhausting, and although the result had apparently not been positive in terms of sales, it had been a great learning experience for me and for everyone at Henco. From then on, we have tried to be much more measured in our emotions, neither all the joy nor all the sadness. This is what happens in life:

when you get what you want, it's okay to be happy, but without pushing it; likewise, when you don't get it, it's okay to be sad or angry, but also without pushing it.

I have always thought that life is constant growth and one must play between these two lines, without falling into euphoria or depression. Whenever you get euphoric and go over the top, you're likely to get a little depressed afterwards. And when you fall into depression, you get stuck with that feeling; the longer you stay there, the harder it is to get yourself out.

Another lesson I learned from this experience was that I could not do things alone. I thought I was Superman, Batman, and Spider-Man all in one. When I realized that carrying all the responsibilities of the company on my shoulder was robbing me of happiness, I focused on sharing them. More people needed to be empowered, their skills cultivated and made to grow so that they too would feel fulfilled, successful, and happy. If Henco takes care of its people, people will take care of Henco, I thought. So, my team became my priority.

Walking on the path to happiness does not just mean that you want to be happy; happiness is achieved when you make others feel good. You can have the Commandments up on your wall, repeat mantras, but people will forget what they've heard. Only that which touches their hearts remains with them.

In business, as in life, it all comes down to how you make people feel. It's that easy and that hard.

Today, I dare say that success depends on knowing how to build happiness in companies. Thousands of years ago, a successful person was the one who had more slaves; later, the one who made slaves work harder; after the Industrial Revolution, the one who had more machines; later, the one who controlled information; a few decades later, the one who knew how to give value to big data; today, it is the sum of the above, plus the control of artificial intelligence. I maintain that the companies of the future must stand out for their humanism, the way they treat their people, and whoever has the biggest heart will win. The most human enterprise will be the most successful.

Henco has managed to grow at its own pace and be part of a difficult industry. We use the same boats and planes as our competitors. What sets us apart is the way we do it: smiling and with a positive attitude. Logistics is complex. Handling international freight, air, sea, land, import, and export cargo from all corners of the world is a hard and relentless task, a 24/7 job. In a conversation with my team, customers and suppliers asked me what made us different, to which I replied: "Henco is a happy company that also happens to work in logistics."

Making customers happy in this industry is no small feat. You have to be attentive to solving their problems, to have everything under control within a positive work environment, with a lot of social awareness, absolute willingness to serve, loyalty, and honesty as your foundations. Making people proud to work at Henco, to serve our customers and to make their lives easier, is all about building happiness, and achieving this requires constant discipline and commitment.

As a result of this discipline and this consistency, we received the award for the best logistics company to work for in Mexico, by Great Place to Work Institute, and have held on to the distinction ten years in a row.

The bottom line is that we want to be happy, and that should be the rule, not the exception. I want more companies to get this kind of award because it reflects a real change in work culture. Not because of an award per se, but because I really want more people to live a fulfilled life. When I talk about more people, I mean customers, suppliers, competitors, and their families, in this and in all industries.

It doesn't mean that everything at Henco is perfect. It means that we will 'go all out' to do a better job and deliver your products properly, in a timely manner, and at a reasonable cost. The moment we make our clients shine, they will feel good, and in turn, they'll take care of us. And it works down the whole chain: everyone has to be satisfied with what they get from Henco.

How can we always guarantee that satisfaction? Be ready for the unexpected and be very flexible. For example, one of Henco's services is hand carriers. In other words, we have to be faster than the fastest courier, and the only way to achieve this is by getting a person on the plane to get anywhere in the world in a matter of hours.

One Saturday night, at 9 PM, I received an unusual call: a client in León, Guanajuato, had been bitten by a poisonous snake, and after searching all over Mexico for the antidote, they realized that there was none available. They found a dose in San José, Costa Rica, which required permits and transfer. We did everything in our power. The life of a human being was at stake, and in a few hours, with almost perfectly coordinated logistics, we managed to deliver the antidote to the client, and he was saved. What a deep satisfaction for those of us involved in that delivery!

Another example of always being ready and flexible came a few years later. Another call: "We have six screws in Mexico that we need to deliver immediately to Cairo, Egypt. How fast can you get them there?", a customer asked me. At that time, it was about 36 hours with the fastest packaging service. We found someone in the company who could fly immediately with their documents in order, bought a ticket, and had him fly across the world. This is where we apply High Performance, Happy People. We delivered in 16 hours –High Performance– and, as a reward for their good work on this and many other deliveries, we invited our partner to stay on as a tourist in Egypt for a week-Happy People. That's the human side of Henco.

We wake up every day with a limited amount of energy. It's life and we can't help it. How we use that energy is up to us. You decide whether you use it to build a full life and transmit it to others, or use it to fight, argue, offend, and destroy. By law, energy is neither created nor destroyed, it is only transformed.

Let's transform the energy that life gives us into positive things because this is real life! We don't have another one; life is not a rehearsal.

FULFILLED

HIGH PERFORMANCE
HAPPY PEOPLE

No matter how educated, talented, rich or powerful you are, the way you treat people says it all.

SIMON COHEN
CAP 06

There's no real success without happiness. And to be happy, all you have to do is decide to be. Like many others, I have found the greatest sense of peace and fulfillment in my family, so I wanted to bring those deep emotions of loyalty and connection to our corporate culture and make my team a family.

My brothers' contributions have been fundamental to the success of the company. And the values we share are a direct result of our parents' legacy: both my mother and father taught us the value of hard work and embracing opportunities.

That's why we decided to change the name of the company when we acquired all the shares. We used the syllables that form the Cohen surname as a reminder that this is a business with strong family roots, but changed the order (Hen-Co) as a way to reinvent the concept and be inclusive. We have always wanted everyone who works with us to feel part of Henco, no matter what their last name happens to be.

Since Henco was born, we have strived to offer its employees the experience of belonging to a big family. This can only be achieved by sharing successes and challenges, developing human relationships, creating wellbeing, and caring for people in an honest way.

Implementing a culture of wellbeing, **FULFILLMENT**, and happiness, which simultaneously stimulates productivity and greater performance, required a lot of work. But from a young age, I learned that effort unites people, the same as in a sports team. You can't be happy when you're hungry or cold; the better you perform, the happier you are, and the happier you are, the better you perform. It's a virtuous circle.

Thus was born what would soon become the basis of Henco's organizational culture: High Performance, Happy People. If you can't be happy at work, which is where you spend most of your waking hours, then what is the meaning of life?

It is practically impossible to have a fulfilled life if you are not happy in your work.

Not only do I thank American Airlines (AA) for the many trips they allowed Tammy and me to make at the beginning of our marriage, I also received great indirect lessons from the company.

The first lesson came on a day that we needed to return from Paris to Mexico for work. There was room on the plane, so we practically had our seats secured.

Within the employee travel policy, there was a dress code: formal clothing and dress shoes. As on every trip, we dressed according to the rules.

That day, when I tried to board, the boarding pass collector looked me up and down, and plainly said I couldn't get on the plane because I hadn't followed dress protocol. We didn't understand what he was talking about. A blazer and a pair of dress pants exceeded the requirements. What was the problem?

It turned out that my loafers without laces had seemed too informal to the person who was greeting the passengers. Just like that. The loafers made me miss a flight, which, in turn, made me late to work. I knew that day that I didn't want to be like that employee, who had also reproached us for traveling 'without paying', when in fact, the flights were not a gift but a benefit that my wife received for being an employee of the airline. "Not only are you traveling for free, you also want to travel the way you want to", he scolded us.

Once again, I decided to turn a bad moment into a positive lesson: in the face of any adversity and especially when it comes to helping my clients, I would look for the best solution, something that would benefit them first, and therefore, benefit us all. Since then, every time an obstacle arises, I ask, "How can we help?", and we look for all possible scenarios before drawing on a "not possible."

No matter what we do, we have all been someone's client and have experienced the frustration of dealing with people who are unwilling, arrogant, and want to feel some kind of power over us because they're not happy with their lives. The feeling of power gives them some satisfaction without thinking about how much it affects others. This is what it means to be a bureaucrat. When you're frustrated in your life, you seek to crush people in your work to feel a degree of satisfaction and power. Nothing could be further from what we seek at Henco! Our aim is to be a flexible company while maintaining control.

When they're born, babies are very physically flexible, they can touch their head with their feet without much effort. As they grow, they get greater control over their body. In youth, they have similar amounts of flexibility and control, representing our peak of physical potential as humans. When we're adults, we start losing flexibility, but have absolute control of our body. The same happens with companies. When they are born, they are malleable, and as time goes by, they lose this flexibility and gain in control. Excessive control is bureaucracy. The magic is in keeping the balance between the two. Ever since I heard my teacher Ichak Adizes give this example, I understood that the intersection of those two lines on a graph was the place where I wanted to keep Henco.

People who hurt or offend you don't necessarily think about the impact that action will have on you. Many times, they do these things to fill a void they have, because of some turmoil in their lives. We must feel empathy, always think positively, and understand that we know nothing about what is going on in the lives of others. We cannot get angry because a taxi driver cut us off on the way to the office or someone looked at us funny on the street. It makes your day bitter, and they walk away like nothing happened. Don't let them throw their 'garbage' at you: react with a smile, and know that everyone is fighting a battle that you know nothing about, so ALWAYS be kind. A smile is the most powerful weapon in the world. Even though we were not allowed to travel that day in Paris, Tammy and I smiled and thanked this person. Our hearts were at peace, and again, the phrase "everything happens for a reason, for something good" came to mind. We didn't have to be on that plane.

I've extracted many other lessons from American Airlines. You learn from everything if you're alert to the messages that life sends! Tammy would come home every night and tell me something she thought was good or not so good about the company, and I would apply it or try to improve upon it at Henco. Unwittingly, AA turned out to be one of my greatest sources of inspiration in generating a culture of change in our company. There was no comparison in size and scope, but we were already taking small steps on safe ground. Another lesson was to realize that humility includes being open to receiving lessons from others. It is always possible to learn from mistakes and successes.

Tammy told me one day that her boss had started the day in a bad mood and didn't say good morning to anyone. The next morning, I showed up at Henco with a smile on my face and greeted anyone who crossed my path. If she told me that the bathrooms in her office were dirty, I would hold a meeting to ask that the bathrooms always be sparkling clean. If she told me that fellow employees were complaining about not getting paid for parking, next month, we would offer free parking to everyone at Henco.

It went the same way with positive things, like when she told me about the 'Ring the Bell' strategy, which consisted of ringing a bell every time someone reached a sales' target. The psychological and motivational effect that you get from doing something symbolic when you conquer a goal is incredible. Those who 'rang the bell' for Henco had a huge smile of satisfaction, which grew with the applause and cheers from others. It is important to strive to reach the goal, and also to inspire others to fight and rejoice when someone else succeeds, because everyone benefits. That's our team concept. As the African proverb goes: "If you want to go fast, go alone; if you want to go far, go with others."

We were still a small company but we had the best intentions, including offering challenges and recognition to our workers and, above all, many moments of happiness to those who worked there. The central idea, long before our High Performance, Happy People methodology was developed, was that every morning we would come back to the office with more enthusiasm than the previous day. The results on a personal and business level were increasingly clear. We understood that investing in the happiness of others is investing in your own happiness.

Life is too short to be happy only on the weekend.

Just like at swim training, when I was asked to project my goals into the future, I visualized where I wanted to take the company. From the beginning, I knew that personal relationships and constructive treatment of my colleagues had to be a fundamental part of Henco's competitive advantage. Having happy employees means having satisfied customers and, consequently, positive results.

High Performance, Happy People is a virtuous circle that is built on three pillars: Wellness (sleeping well, eating healthy, and exercising), Mindfulness (meditation, spiritual connection, gratitude), and Happiness (enjoying life, family, friends, giving, inspiring). With this, and working every day with respect and trust, you are taking the first step to happiness and success. As a consequence of having these three pillars in balance, you will be a high-performance person.

At Henco, we encourage people to work towards having good habits. People don't decide their future, they decide their habits; and their habits define their future. We also make sure that their personal life goes well. I always tell them: "Give your best and never forget to enjoy it." A positive culture translates into improvements in talent recruitment, greater staff retention, and increased commitment and productivity of those who work with you.

Only by ensuring that employees are properly engaged in their personal lives do they truly develop the best of their talents. If you have stability in your personal life, you can be stable in your work life.

Culture is not something that is imposed or taught, that's the challenge: it is something alive, organic. Of course, we have an orientation course for new employees, but we believe High Performance, Happy People must be born from within, to the degree that you feel a part of Henco.

One study we did points out that good or bad practices spread quickly amongst people. It is important to detect the 'bad apples' in time, the people who always complain, that no matter how much of an effort you make, they think everything is wrong and spread their energy in a toxic way within the company and within the team.

When they are identified by the employees themselves, the 'bad apples' feel uncomfortable, and end up joining the team and changing their attitude, or leaving the company.

It is an ecosystem in which people take care of each other: if your work makes you happy because it is well paid; if you have quality time; there is space so that your colleagues care about you being well in all aspects of your life –Wellness, Mindfulness, and Happiness– you will not want to lose this, you will take care of it more and more. When people feel good, supported, loved, and valued, they are more motivated and appreciate their work. Therefore, it is Henco's collaborators who make sure no one interrupts this harmony. Without claiming to be perfect, the formula works.

The worst thing you can do is run away from work to find happiness. Laziness will never fill that void. Doing intense and fun work with the best attitude will make you truly happy.

At Henco, people are accepted as they are, regardless of sexual preference, gender, nationality, or skin color. We want everyone to feel comfortable and happy. Trust is natural here. Our culture is based on supporting each other.

We encourage people to find a balance between their work and personal lives. We tell them, first and foremost, you are a mother or father, sister, brother, daughter or son, and then you are a part of this team. We understand that we have to take care of the important people in our lives.

Every employee is a human being who loves their children as much as I love mine. When you understand that we are all equal and that we have feelings, you build a very different relationship with people, not just with employees, but also with clients, suppliers, and even with competitors. Our objective is not to be the biggest; that will be the consequence, if we do the job right. Our goal is to be the best at what we do and to spread happiness.

We inspire our people to think this way because if they are doing well in their personal lives, they'll do well at Henco. If they are at work but busy in their minds with a personal problem, they will not be productive. Our philosophy includes giving them time and support to solve personal situations and then return to the office to be efficient.

And not only when they have problems, but also when there are important moments to share with their loved ones. This became very clear to me one time I was late to the office after attending the Mother's Day festival at my daughter's school. I was telling Héctor, the first person who worked with me at Henco, about what my little girl had done during the show, and amidst laughter about the story, he said, "How nice that you were able to go and see her!" He has a daughter almost the same age as mine. I asked him when her school festival would be. He said, "It was today." In shock and feeling guilty, I asked him why he hadn't gone. To which he replied, "I didn't go because it was during office hours." I froze.

Why, if I have the chance to enjoy that special moment with my daughter, can't my coworker? Since then, I tell everyone, "If I have the right to attend my daughters' Mother's Day festival, or the final game of my kids' soccer tournament, so do you. We all have the right to take care of our personal lives and spend time with our families." These freedoms are a right and a responsibility. I have never left any work pending while attending these events, and the same goes for them. It's a sign of maturity.

Being physically well –Wellness– is the basis for high performance. Nutrition is the first premise that we try to take care of. Food is our gasoline. If we fill the tank with junk, we will not have the energy to run properly. At Henco, we guide our people and encourage them to have positive eating habits. Without it being an obligation, we provide them with information that makes them understand the benefits of healthy eating.

Sleep regenerates the cells of our body; there's nothing more important than that! We have to learn to rest in order to have energy and give our best. Arianna Hufftington often talks about the importance of getting a good night's sleep, which she considers a treasure. Justin Trudeau, being the prime minister of a country, asks his staff to let him rest at least eight hours a night. If a busy man such as Trudeau can, why can't we?

The basketball player LeBron James bases his high-performance routine on rest. He says that if someone offered you a drink that would restart your body, balance your emotions, put you in a better mood, recharge your mind so you'd be more creative and productive, and boost your immune system so you wouldn't get sick often, wouldn't you drink it? I would! Because all these benefits are scientifically proven, and sleep is free. All you need to do is spend eight hours a day on it.

This is what sleep does. The challenge is that it takes

time. You have to put all other things on pause: responsibilities, relationships, projects, work, friends, family. Everything. Hours in a day are finite. Time spent awake is very valuable, but for this time to be valuable, you need your sleep. The hours you spend sleeping are an investment, every minute you put into it gives a return of two minutes of the best version of you. It's an incredible return! As a good friend says, "I don't sleep much, I sleep slowly."

Oxygenating our cells is also essential. By exercising consistently, we get blood flowing and bring oxygen to the brain. I have no doubt that it is essential to cleanse our organism and generate endorphins which, in turn, generate a feeling of happiness. Being mentally well –Mindfulness– allows you to have clarity. Spiritual connection, whatever your beliefs or religion, brings you a peace of mind that helps you make better decisions and eliminate stress. We suggest meditation as a tool to achieve this connection and provide a space for our employees to do so, or to simply sit and be silent. Stress is a constant in our industry and we often repeat to ourselves:

Stop trying to calm the storm. Find your own calm, give your best, and the storm will pass.

Sometimes the secret to being at peace is having a bad memory. We cannot –and should not– be drawing out and remembering the problems of the past with the people around us. What happened, happened, and there's nothing we can do to change it, only learn. They say that a person is intelligent if they learn from others' mistakes. Being at peace is a state of mind that requires full conviction of really wanting it, regardless of the bad times that everyone goes through.

When you focus on the good, the good becomes extraordinary.

The third pillar is Happiness. In our idea of a **FULFILLED** life, laughter, friends, and good times cannot be missing. We have to give ourselves space and time to enjoy ourselves and laugh a little. I'm sure that our culture based on people's happiness has been fundamental in achieving the goals we set for ourselves as a company. Even after several years, many people who have worked at Henco have kept in touch. What they appreciate most is that during their time with the company, they made some of their best friends here. It's another way in which we're leaving our mark.

High Performance, Happy People is the sum of small daily actions. From the moment someone new arrives at the company, we try to make sure that there are small gestures that make them feel welcome, at home. We all say hello, we all say goodbye. It's very simple. We laugh and share unusual experiences from our work and personal lives. A chocolate, a coffee, a thank you note. Giving is a way of life at Henco.

When I made the changes to make Henco look and actually be a happy place, I knew that I had to build our foundations on values. I don't want the values at our company to exist just for keynotes and websites. At Henco, our values have to go hand in hand with our vision and why we exist. Passion, high performance, and of course, happiness, were and still are our starting point.

For example, at the 'Hencongresos' that we have been organizing for more than 15 years, we do not focus only on business talk. The first thing on the agenda is personal growth. We prepare an activity in which we highlight Henco's values, and every night there is an event to thank everyone for their attendance and for the work we do together.

We have a speaker on self-improvement; life testimonies that make us value what we have. We try to 'infect' our guests with our values so that they too can have a **FULFILLED** life. In no way do we downplay the topics of logistics and transportation, which come after we connect with people and raise their awareness.

Every year, we take groups of more than 200 people to the container port terminals that, for obvious reasons, are not in the most 'touristy' parts of our country. We bring together clients, shipping companies, port terminal personnel, government authorities, inland carriers, customs agents, and even competitors, at places such as Lázaro Cárdenas, Michoacán, or Manzanillo, Colima.

On these trips together, we learn to meditate, exercise, eat well, and we also talk about logistics. While the events are a networking opportunity, we also make sure that there are personal surprises and that we touch the hearts of the attendees. One time, for example, we asked the relatives of each person there to record a video message of gratitude and acknowledgement to surprise them. We all arrived on time at 9 PM, where an incredible buffet was set up on the sand. The sound of the sea and the background music set the perfect stage for our gift. When dinner was over, we spoke a few words and projected the video with beautiful, emotional music. As we watched, fireworks filled the sky with light and color. Many of the attendees were moved to tears.

My idea is that for a few minutes everyone have the same feeling of fullness that I had that night at the beach with Tammy and my daughters; that they feel acknowledged by their loved ones, and this motivates them to keep growing and improving. People will be happy if we acknowledge their value as human beings and how indispensable they are to the company.

In one of those meetings in Manzanillo, something happened that struck me. Since we founded the company, I have always made it a point to get to know the people I work with –there is nothing better than calling them by their name. I take that practice with me everywhere I go, from a restaurant to when I fly. I always glance at the nametag and call people by their name. It's a very simple thing, but it has a big impact.

That night, I was the motivational speaker. My speech had touched the audience and I was very pleased with the outcome. There was a moment when I shed a few tears and it spread to the audience. When I finished, I went to my assigned table for dinner and warmly greeted those who were already sitting there. The woman next to me thanked me and said that what I had just said about happiness touched her heart and she was willing to make changes in her life to reach fulfillment. She kept praising me. I thanked her deeply for her words and after looking at her nametag, I called her by name and asked her: “Mariana, what company do you work for?” She replied with a half-hearted and surprised smile: “At Henco, going on a year.”

It was a shock and a huge miss. I really didn’t remember seeing her, and between the noise of the music and the dimmed lights, I recognized her even less. How was that possible? I was running a company with a philosophy of community and closeness and I, as a leader, had just made this mistake. It was a wake-up call. I had to react, and I decided to double my efforts to get to know the people who work at Henco. No matter how many we are, what matters is to always maintain the human touch that makes us different.

This episode led us to form small teams, create opportunities for more leaders with a short chain of command, and thus perpetuate closeness and the open-door policy that characterizes Henco.

We are committed to listening to all ideas, regardless of the level from which they come. In the planning meetings that we organize every year, all the company problems are raised, and we begin to dream. We shut ourselves down for three or four days, and this is where the best ideas come up on how to change customer service, how to respond to things, how to make a better operating system, how to design software that fits with High Performance, Happy People, how to do home office or how to make things more fun at Henco.

I shaped the company's human talent policy and organizational culture, which is our identity, but it was my collaborators who made it a reality: them, not me. I'm just another change agent, they're the ones who do everything. I can't force them to laugh during the day, it has to be genuine and natural, otherwise it doesn't work.

"This is a great place to work... not a great place to slack off," is what I tell them. We should not confuse a culture of happiness with license to not work, because we would face a conflict there. That's why High Performance comes before Happy People. High performance is something we can teach; being happy with what you do is the consequence.

This happens not just at 'Hencongresos'. Our day-to-day life is the same: meetings usually begin with little snickers that sometimes turn into peals of laughter. Instead of making a formal introduction, we joke around for the first few minutes, but then, when the meeting officially starts, everything is very efficient. Nobody is there to improvise. It is possible to have a relaxed atmosphere combined with high performance.

We have a couple of consultants that I love –one was born in India and the other one is Mexican– who are some of the smartest people I know. Their way of analyzing situations has always impressed me; in fact, they were the ones who helped us put a name to our High Performance, Happy People philosophy.

The first day they joined a planning meeting, and after the initial minutes of laughter and noise, they caught my attention and asked me for a minute outside the room. "Simon, we're very worried, what is this? People won't stop laughing, we won't get anything done." I said, "Dear friends, give us time. When we get to the work, we'll do it better than anyone. It's part of our culture, trust me." When we got back, I told people, "Let's start the meeting." And, although we never stopped laughing, we switched into 'work mode' and moved ahead quickly. When the meeting was over, they came up to me and said, "It's been a long time since our stomachs hurt from laughing so hard, our jaws are cramped! We really enjoy working with you. We have never seen a strategic planning sheet as good as the one we created today."

Work and good humor are not at odds. It's one thing to be in a bad mood and another to be focused. When we have to focus, we do it one hundred percent, but without losing our humor. How do you dream better: when you are in a good mood, inspired, singing, or when you are in a bad mood, serious, and angry? We must create the perfect environment, the optimal space for people to express themselves in the right way, without offending anyone, with confidence, with respect, but enjoying it! When people are happy, they can work miracles.

We are always going to teach anyone who works at Henco everything and anything, and they have to put in a lot of effort and perform very well to achieve that high performance. We're back to the issue of attitude. We hire the team based on the attitude each of them has –everything else we can teach. Logistics is not rocket science. The best way to learn is wanting to do so. If results happen and we grow, we can give more, share more; we will all be satisfied. Those who do their job very well will also have more time for themselves, to enjoy with their family and more opportunities to travel to see the world, among other things.

A lot of people have said to me, "You changed my life!" I say to them, "And you changed mine!" An organization must be high-performing, but with a lot of heart. Henco is a company full of humans who are very human.

Happiness is the new rich, inner peace is the new success, health is the new wealth, and education, respect, and values are the coolest thing ever!

It's no longer acceptable to pick on people nor to bully, it's not funny to make fun of others, it's not OK to make fun of people because of their sexual preferences or religion. Today, being polite is what is most valued –we have to make it trendy! Goodness is the new cool. Let us all celebrate together acts of kindness, of inclusion, of joy. At Henco, we care about people for the simple fact that they are people, because it is people who make great things happen. Together, we have no limits!

FULFILLED

LET'S KEEP **LEAVING A MARK**

You don't build a business.
You build the people, and then the people build the business.

SIMON COHEN
CAP 07

Over the years, I've met successful people with very complicated life stories, people who have lost everything from material things to the people they most love. They have given me the greatest lessons in resilience. I have heard many of them say, "I have been through very tough things, and that's exactly what makes me who I am", and each of them has been an example and an inspiration. Happiness, more than being a simple visual and physical act, is enjoying your journey, including its darkest moments, and continually looking for new reasons to be happy. The way you react in your most difficult moments defines how you make your way to success.

As I've said before, the ultimate purpose of our life is to seek happiness, both in our personal lives and in the way that we conduct business. From the moment we are born, our actions are focused on finding pleasure: physical, emotional, and spiritual. It is a natural part of being human. But when we look for pleasure, why are there times in which we don't find it? Even worse, we end up facing frustration. I think it has to do with the attitude with which we face problems. "The world breaks everyone and afterward many are strong at the broken places", as Ernest Hemingway said.

This applies both in the business and the personal realms. At Henco, we try to understand the reason for what we do, we strive to give meaning to the products we move, a purpose. It changes our perspective on things and gives a sense of meaning to our daily work.

There is a story about three construction workers building the same building, who are then asked what they were doing. The first one bitterly says he merely stacks bricks. The second one answers simply that he's building a wall. The third worker, who found meaning in what he was doing, answers, "I am building the most beautiful cathedral in the world." That's what we need to understand. Why do you work, what's the ultimate goal, what do you want to see happen with what you're doing? Making sense of what you do changes the way you look at things.

That is precisely what we seek at Henco. We're not just transporting boxes, pallets, and containers –we move hope, dreams, and joy. When we see a child in a park playing with her bike, we feel proud –we are part of her smile. When we see a doctor dressed in the medical equipment we deliver, we feel like part of the cure. Even when we go to the supermarket and see the aisles full of products transported by Henco, we feel that we are feeding the world.

We've seen buildings and thought, "Can you imagine? Windows, furniture, aluminum, flooring, bathroom fixtures, we moved it all!" And there are lots of things that evoke the same feeling in us: schools, hospitals, streets, factories with specialized ovens, breweries, restaurants. We're a part of their story. Almost everything inside was also carried there by Henco: books, medicine, clothes, cars, planes, even trains –we move just about everything. But, I insist, we don't see it as cargo tonnage or airborne kilograms; we always find meaning in what we do.

Logistics can be very stressful if you don't put heart into it. We do logistics with a human touch.

We don't just do this internally, but externally as well. A few years ago, in an effort to make even more sense out of what we do, we started the 'Henconciencia' Foundation. It is managed by the company's own employees and our end goal is to help those who need it the most.

One day, while we were touring the port terminal of Lázaro Cárdenas as part of a 'Hencongreso', I noticed a young woman at her desk crying. Since I had already made this trip several times, I let our guests continue with the tour, and I approached her: "What's wrong, why are you crying?" I asked her. She didn't want to answer me at first, so I insisted: "Don't worry, whatever your problem is, everything will be fine. Everything has a solution, except for death." To which she replied, "That's just it." I went pale, and she continued: "My four-year-old nephew has just been diagnosed with a terminal illness called Wiskott-Aldrich." I had no idea what this was. Without knowing anything else about her life and after talking for only a couple of minutes, I assured her: "We'll help you. That child is not going to die."

She said that the biggest obstacle was the amount of money required to treat it, and because she came from a low-income family, they would never be able to get it. Not only did Ramoncito have this disease, but the spinal cord match he needed for the transplant was not in Mexico. There was just the one donor and he was in Europe.

I asked her to give us time and promised we would soon get in touch with her. After the convention was over, I met with Henco's team and told them what had happened. "We have to save Ramoncito", I told them. And they all said that we'd do our best to make it happen. I learned this from my mother: help others without expecting anything in return. So, we got to work.

In the span of a few months, we organized fundraising activities. Each and every one of Henco's collaborators invested time and effort to raise the money needed. From selling snacks, to holding raffles and other activities on weekends. Clients and suppliers joined the cause and made special donations. When we finally reached the amount, we invited Ramoncito and his family to our offices. In an emotional moment, surrounded by all those who had contributed and struggled to fulfill this dream, we symbolically handed over the funds. The money went straight to payment for treatment. It's been a while, and from that day on, each year on my birthday, Ramoncito sends me a video thanking us for what we did for him and congratulating me. I still have all the videos, and hold most dear a drawing that he made for me on the day of his surgery, of superheroes covering the page and atop it, in his child-like handwriting, he wrote: "Henco is a superhero."

Happy employees will not only better serve the needs of a company's clients, but they will see their work as not just another job and as an extension of the culture, of being part of a family focused on doing good for others with vision and aligned values.

High Performance, Happy People is our mantra. The outcome of the company's caring about its team is that the team will in return care about the company, about what we have created together. When you give people security, the inevitable result is profit.

In a society that is broken and lacking values, it's difficult to understand what it means to give someone security, to protect them, to say: "I will take care of you and you will take care of me." The more I give you, the more you take care of me, the more I help you, the more you help me. It's like a paying-it-forward dynamic that grows exponentially. I'm sure it works. That is why when the Covid-19 pandemic hit, we made an important decision: to take care of our peoples' jobs.

We had a virtual meeting with the team and promised that nobody would lose their job because, just as they have given themselves body and soul to the company, once again Henco was going to take care of them, to protect them with all its might so that their salaries would not be affected. The outcome? Higher productivity indicators.

We implemented home office and our bond was stronger than ever. If you use real actions to prove to your team that you are going to take care of them, without a doubt they'll reciprocate. The exceptional response we had from our employees and friends was impressive. I can only thank them and say again that I would never turn my back on them after everything they have done for the company.

And it's not just about money. If we are disciplined, it is easier to achieve goals and get positive results. The issue is how to be empathetic with people, how to build those alliances. I am fortunate enough to work in an industry where I interact with people from all over the world. My daughters find it funny because they say that wherever we go I have friends, even in the most random places, and it's true! When we travel in Mexico and other countries, there is always someone we know who we'll meet for dinner or who invites us to visit them at their home; sometimes I'll just bump into someone right there on the street.

Interpersonal relationships are the best; it's what I enjoy the most. What I mean is networking around the world and creating links to learn from people, their cultures, have fun and, why not, to do some business. Regardless if it's for a Henco-related matter or not, when I meet someone, my first thought is not what I can get from that person as a businessman. The first thing that comes to my mind is: "What can I learn from this person?" The next thing is, "What can I do for this person, what can I contribute to their life?" If I can answer those questions, the rest just comes to me, whether it's friendship, business, or both. The only way to answer these questions is by talking and, most importantly, showing a lot of interest in what the other person is saying.

When one teaches, two learn.

Body language reveals a lot about a person, and I believe that, to make the most of a conversation, one has to bring full attention to the table. Every time I talk to someone, I try to forget about my cell phone, the computer, my thoughts, and open myself up to that moment.

As I've said, listening carefully is the best way to learn from others. Exchanging ideas with others is an investment of time, and time is precious.

The biggest difference between money and time, is that you can know how much money you have, but you will never know how much time you have left.

If you manage to create deep bonds, if your networking is a constant and reciprocal effort, people become mirrors that allow you to see who you are. If you're open and willing to look for ways to help others, you will get that open willingness in return. It's not about doing things expecting to receive the exact same thing in return, but about acknowledging your growth as a human being through the simple act of giving. What you get is an extra. By giving, you've already gained.

That is why friendship is one of my most valued treasures, and my life story has allowed me to have friends from all over the world, with very different traditions and ways of seeing life. We have always found middle ground because human beings possess specific characteristics that are not determined by place of birth, the religion you profess, or the political party you support. If these differences are based on respect and empathy, they become very powerful connections.

If you focus on helping others grow, you grow. If you focus on the problems, the problems grow.

During the time I spent at Harvard presenting on our case study, I met an important Turkish businessman with whom I had the opportunity to spend time for several days. We talked a lot, we shared our life stories as people and as businessmen, and in no time we became good friends. By the end of the week, he gave me what he had written about our case and said, "I feel very fortunate to have heard about your experience firsthand. Listening to you made me see how lucky I am to have found such an incredible person in my life." He then quoted the Dalai Lama: "Taking care of others, helping others, ultimately is the way to discover your own joy and to have a happy life." That's what I call 'wise selfishness' he said, and continued, "You are the most 'intelligent selfish' person I have ever known." His words sent a shiver down my spine. A person I admire so much and have so much to learn from realized that my focus was on others, and he acknowledged that.

This is what I mean when I say that people can become your mirror. And it's not about the mirror exclusively reflecting the positive or flattering side. The people who love you will have the courage to point out your flaws and have the patience to help you correct them. As my father-in-law Nemo always says when we ask his opinion about something: "Do you want me to say what you want to hear, or what I really think?" The people who love you the most will praise you as well as guide you towards a better path.

For me, the best way to start any relationship is with a smile. When I have dealt with people who speak a language that I don't understand much of, I stick to the saying, "Everyone smiles in the same language." When I arrive at a meeting, wherever and with whomever, my business card is always a sincere smile. That's where it all begins.

Charlie Chaplin used to say: "A smile costs nothing but gives much. It enriches those who receive it without making poorer those who give it. It takes but a moment, but the memory of it sometimes lasts forever."

And if smiling is a universal language, it is certainly also a very powerful weapon, and best of all, it's free! All you need to have is the intention to give it away. It's included in the package since birth, but not all of us have learned to use it, even though its effects are immediate and expansive.

A smile is a weapon that disarms.

Is something I often say. If you give it to someone who's having a bad day, you can turn their day right around. Smiling is one of the most contagious things that exist.

It's not about going through life with a permanent smile plastered on your face or about faking it. Smiling sincerely to the world is one way to show your resilience and to be grateful for what you do have. The people who smile the most are not always those with the least problems, but the ones who manage to see the good things more than or in spite of the bad ones.

It's also not about posting smiling photos of yourself, showing the world where you are and how well you are eating, in search of acceptance. It's about being genuine, enjoying the moment, and that may include a smile. We live in increasingly visual times, in which we ache for each other's approval every waking moment, which often connects us on a merely superficial level while disconnecting us from our purpose. Technology brings us closer to those who are far away and distances us from those who are near.

Today, our pace of life has changed: everything is done in a hurry. We're worried, tired, and often we don't take the time to look at others, let alone stop and gift them with a smile. Let's make a habit of it, like saying good morning or thank you: smiling is still the best garnish in any conversation, in person or at a distance.

Beyond the technology that already exists and what is to come, I prefer direct contact with people. While I believe that no one escapes social media, in my opinion the best 'Like' I can give someone else is my smile and my attention. Screens have eaten away at a part of our reality. How about try this out? Start at home. Pay attention to others, no distractions, smile, ask questions: people want to tell their story, and there is always something to learn in personal stories.

I apply this philosophy in my leadership style. There are three stages in becoming a good leader: the first is to give your best; the second is to learn that when you are present, you bring out the best version of your teammates; and the third is that this behavior prevails in your absence.

A good leader has to be an example, a passionate person. Passion is incredibly contagious, it produces wonderful energy. Passion is not a state of mind, but a way of being.

I learned this when I was barely 15 years old and firmly decided to quit swimming. I was tired and bored, parties and friends were calling to me. Swimming is a very 'jealous' sport and cannot be combined with any of these, so I chose to go the easy way –to have fun and to do what most people my age were doing.

When my teammates and coaches found out, I got calls from most of them trying to persuade me that the best was yet to come and that I shouldn't quit the team. One of them, Juan Carlos, took matters into his own hands. On the third day of me not showing up for practice, he turned up at my house. After chatting a bit, he said: "Eight years ago you came to train for the first time as part of this team that we have been a part of for so long. That day I asked you why you had switched teams, and you said that one day you wanted to go to the Olympics and that the best swimmers were training here. We promised each other right there that we would go to the Olympics together. You can't back out. We either go together or neither of us goes at all." It was a silly little promise between two seven-year-olds, but Juan Carlos was taking it very seriously now.

After that conversation, he would show up at my house every day and insist that I shouldn't jump ship, that we had to go through the whole process together. "If you're not going to train, neither am I", Juan Carlos kept saying.

I felt that the more time passed, the more I hurt him. “You go on, I don’t want to do this anymore. This is it for me as an athlete. You have to reach your goal”, I said. At that time, he was at his peak as a swimmer and had a promising future. “No way am I going alone, we have to keep our promise to each other.” He was so persistent that he convinced me. I went back to training and that’s when my best years in swimming arrived.

This is an example of a passionate leader who does not stop until he accomplishes what’s best for the other person, even if the cost is to sacrifice himself: two weeks of not training could have made a huge difference between winning or losing. After a couple of years, and because of this attitude, Juan Carlos was named captain of the college team. Although neither of us achieved our goal of the Olympics, the journey was so enriching that not for one second do we regret having walked that path together. To this day, he is one of my best friends.

Leadership must be proven by truly living our values more than anyone else, so that there is no doubt that what you say is what you do. We leaders have to lead by example, as this story I read and loved from Rabbi Jacobson explains:

One day, two men meet and the younger one asks the older one:

— “Do you remember me?”
— “No.”
— “I was your student and now I’m a teacher.”
— “Why did you decide to become a teacher?”
— Because you inspired me.

One day, in one of your classes, a classmate brought a new watch to show everyone, and I stole it. He noticed the theft and reported it to you. You spoke to the whole class: 'Someone has stolen this boy's watch. Whoever stole it, give it back.' But I didn't want to give it back. You then closed the door and asked us to stand up so that you could search our pockets until you found the watch. You told us to close our eyes and turn to the wall so no one would see you looking.

When you got to me, you found the watch and retrieved it, but kept pretending to look in everyone else's pockets. When you were done, you said, 'You can open your eyes. I found the watch.' You said nothing else. You never outed the culprit. You forever saved my dignity on that day; it was the greatest shame of my life. You gave me an invaluable moral lesson. I got the message: I understood what a true leader should do. Do you remember that moment, professor?"

— "I remember the situation, the stolen watch, and that I went through all the students' pockets. But I didn't remember you because while looking for the watch I closed my eyes too!"

This story is a constant reminder of how we should behave as leaders. It's not the one who shouts the most or imposes his will the most that will gain the most followers, but the one who most inspires, values, and raises others up.

Leaders must have a service-driven attitude, be down-to-earth, and have as their ultimate goal the creation and training of more leaders.

Finally, a good leader has to know how to listen. This requires all their energy, and ironically, it is very easy to pretend that you are paying attention. The only way to become a great listener is to practice. Listening to learn. Because the more you know, the better you will do. Knowing how to think and analyze when we are alone and choosing our words with care when we are with other people.

Think three times as much, listen twice as much, and talk half as much.

It is very clear that Henco is not the biggest nor the best company in the world. We face many challenges, and the potential for growth is considerable. What motivates me to keep going? Why did I dare to write my story when we are a company that still has so much to learn? The answer is simple. I want to leave a legacy of kindness and humanism. Just as someone inspired me, I want to be an inspiration to others.

Given the nature of our industry, at Henco we do business with people from many countries. If we manage to have an influence on one person in every place and they, in turn, manage to convey our philosophy to a family member or friend, then we will be creating a ripple effect of kindness and wellbeing that is greatly needed in our world. I'm not saying that we are the only company that does this. In fact, my first encounter with Francesca Gino, the Harvard professor who wrote our case, was to ask her how I could learn more about a subject we had studied in one of her classes, which talked about a company that treated its employees really well.

I often analyze other peoples' best practices, learn from them, and try to adapt them to Henco's culture. I find inspiration there and try out new things. Afterwards, I again go in search of the next lesson, creating a virtuous circle of knowledge and implementation. My goal here is to inspire others to do the same and thus grow this knowledge spiral and spread happiness and values to as many people as possible.

Triumph is not for the one who knows best, but for the one who surrounds himself with the best companions.

One of the most important symbols in the Middle East is the Hamsa. The representation of the hand shows the five fingers, all different but very close together, which shows that no matter how different we are, when we are united we will always be stronger. I love its meaning because it fits perfectly with my life philosophy. As I said before, I believe that our differences, aptly used, make us stronger.

This is why both in my personal life and at Henco, we do our best to always stay united. Every time I travel to one of our offices, I like to take the time to personally greet each of my co-workers. When I go from the airport to the office, I talk to my assistant and ask her to update me on all important events –new hires, weddings, births, pregnancies, illnesses, difficult times– so I can make sure that, when I talk with them, everyone knows that I am aware of what is going on, in and out of the office. For me, we are all family. Even though we have different personalities and responsibilities, we are united and equal because we all have something to contribute and something to learn.

I find job hierarchies useful exclusively for creating organizational charts. In real life, I love the stories of people who started their working life at the bottom and worked up, because that's my story too. Since I was young, I have always liked to climb and advance in everything I do, and I constantly aim for the highest level. At some point, I set a goal for myself that I continue to pursue today: every year, I add one more line to my resume. I set a goal to do something that is good enough to include in it –both personally and professionally– because I know that will be my legacy.

If there is one thing I am clear about, it is that every person who crosses my path is better at something than I am, and it's a passion for me to find out what that thing is. I remember that even as a child I could detect people's abilities or extraordinary qualities. I liked to analyze them and approach them to learn from them and be better. At school, it was easy for me to spot the smartest students as well as those who were going to excel in sports. I have always liked being surrounded by people who are better than me, from whom I could draw inspiration and grow. To this day, whenever I join a new group, I observe each person and try to learn something from each of them.

To really know and understand someone, you have to go beyond mere appearances, know where they come from, and what their dreams are. As Abraham Lincoln said, "I don't like that man. I must get to know him better." There is always something to learn from people, even if there is no chemistry there in the beginning.

That's why my concept of competition is perhaps a little different. Normally, when we hear that word, we think of someone who seeks to be better than someone else, of the constant struggle so that the other side doesn't win. I don't believe in this. I believe in collaboration, that if we are all part of an industry, the goal must be to make it grow. There is no better way to do that than by sharing, so that whoever listens to you gets the best of it and learns, always learns.

In 2004, when Henco's growth started complicating things, purchasing the company, and my relationship with my parents and brothers, I went to Mauricio, one of my best friends, for advice. I didn't know what to do. I felt adrift. I invited him to lunch and after telling him everything that was happening to me, he told me that his dad was part of a group of businessmen who met every month to learn from each other about their best practices. I was struck by this: imagine belonging to a group where all the people in it are willing to help you without an ulterior motive. I liked the idea and asked him to tell me more.

"You need to surround yourself on the loneliest path there is, which is that of general manager, and what better way to do that than with people who are in the same circumstances as you?", he assured me. Motivated by this, I joined YPO (Young Presidents' Organization). This organization is spectacular. It has given me a lot, and today I owe my being a better person, a better businessman, a better husband, a better son... plus an infinite number of fun and true lifetime friends, to this very group.

Thanks to YPO, I have the pleasure of meeting monthly with five businessmen whom I really admire, to discuss issues of our professional, personal, and family lives. We learn something new at every meeting. During February of every year, we go on a six-day retreat where we each have the task to present an analysis of the previous year and our goals for the year ahead. There is nothing better than sharing your dreams with people who inspire you and who help you measure what you did right or wrong in the last 12 months.

When you express it and write it down, it is no longer just a dream: it becomes a work plan. And so, together, we take stock and evaluate our progress over the next few months. The incredible thing about this is that we don't just deal with business issues; we also analyze ourselves on a personal and family level. We always enjoy a good glass of wine to go with these boundless talks.

These five businessmen are the kind of people who talk to you 'straight up' and without beating around the bush. We celebrate triumphs just as much as we get seriously scolded, when necessary. Today, it is incredibly valuable to find that level of trust in a space where you know that, no matter what happens, you will always get the truth, and above all, you will be unconditionally accompanied.

It was also through YPO that I came to Harvard, one more place where I further confirmed my idea that teamwork is the only way to succeed. Every year, I spend a week there studying most of the day, updating myself on the newest concepts, and learning the latest trends in the business world. This allows me to meet people who are as hungry to learn as I am; people with such a broad view of the world that it forces me to challenge my own limits. We learn about business and good practices, yes, but there is also a very important cultural and emotional exchange. Not to mention the number of collaborative relationships I've forged there. I increasingly admire the power of networking. It is an enormous privilege for me to experience this up close, and I am deeply grateful.

The relationship with the teachers is also very enriching because we are talking about people who have published various books, who are international references in many subjects, and with whom I have the privilege of sharing time to learn as professionals and as individuals. Such is the closeness that is accomplished that, afterwards, I feel comfortable enough to contact them for advice or just to ask how their life is going. This is how I came to understand that continuous learning is also a way to extend your knowledge and your support network. Learning has left me with a broader view of how the world works, and with friends scattered in the most remote places.

From a very young age, I adopted learning as a parallel path to my personal and professional life. I want to learn from everyone, and I want to do it all the time. This has even led me to take part in various boards, where I am surrounded by people that are so capable that every time we get together, I still feel a flutter in my stomach from the excitement. These tables are full of talent. I take a lot of notes and I'm still surprised by the way others analyze and simplify situations. There are days when I leave with 15 pages worth of notes because everything they say is very inspiring to me. If that were not enough, being there allows me to express myself and share my opinion with the same passion as I do elsewhere, being mirrored by people who are much better than me. What more could I ask for?

When we had to form the Henco Board, it was very important that it didn't become a fan club that said yes to all of our decisions. We needed to surround ourselves with analytical people, capable of being objective, and who would always tell us the truth, without stopping to think about whether we liked it or not. If, by asking for others' opinion we seek only applause, no one grows. There's nothing better than to have a Board that includes my father and my two brothers, as well as other people who are part of the industry and who elevate us with their individual experience.

We certainly picked the best. They are individuals who came to the company not just for a strategic or business reason; they are people with whom I have also at some point or another coincided in our way of thinking and on our vision about the happiness of others. All four are incredible professionals who have experience working in Mexico and in other countries, in companies of all sizes, with a broad perspective, but with the wit and instinct to guide us without thinking twice. They are exceptional people who, thanks to their experience, always bring out the best in us and, even better, with an intelligence ten times greater than my own. Being able to learn from them makes me feel **FULFILLED.**

The Board meets in person twice a year for two full days, and four times virtually. Those who live outside of Mexico fly here and we welcome them as if they were coming home, faithfully sticking to our friendship protocol. Before we talk business, we have dinner to catch up on personal issues, then comes the board meeting, and finally, we meet in a call to action, where experts help us define our dreams. And, as it should be when one asks for honesty, not everything is rainbows and butterflies. More than once, we've started out with a plan, a strategy, believing that we're on the right track, and the Board has had the good sense and the grace to tell us: "That's not it." I won't deny that sometimes it's very frustrating, but challenges are born from frustrations. If one asks for an external point of view, it is precisely so that those people can detect everything that is out of our line of sight.

When something is beyond my line of sight, I also go to my brothers and sisters-in-law with whom I have built a very strong relationship. I just adore them all. They're all so different, and with our similarities and differences, they always grace me with great lessons. I see intelligence, tenacity, strength, and passion for the areas in which they work. Since appreciation is something I value greatly, my brothers and sisters-in-law cannot be the exception, so every time they inspire me to do or create something new, I tell them, "Look at what you did, look at what you caused." I think it's very important that those who come to influence your life are aware of their effects. Acknowledging others is one of the easiest ways to approach them.

My nieces and nephews, with all the years that separate us, have also given me incredible lessons. The fact that they feel comfortable enough to call me and tell me about their lives because they trust me as someone who can give them advice, elevates us all. They learn, and with each of their stories, I learn too. I've always thought that it's better to give young people experiences rather than things; this is what I've focused on with them. Memories are something that last a lifetime, and in this way, I carve out quality time to listen to them, to get to know them, learn from them, and create a real bond.

Every person who crosses your path has come to teach you something, and in turn, will take something from you. In order to see this, it's important to keep your eyes open, forget prejudice, and throw yourself fully into getting to know the other person. Really get to know them. Take the best others have to offer to become a better you and leave the best of yourself in others, so that the same thing happens to them. That's why I strive to surround myself with the best, no matter what they do, because I'm very clear on one thing: "If you surround yourself with five reliable people, you will be the sixth; if you surround yourself with five intelligent people, you will be the sixth; if you surround yourself with five fulfilled people, you will be the sixth; if you surround yourself with five negative people, you will be the sixth."

Sometimes we think that being the best means being the richest or the most famous. For me, being the best means doing what you do with passion and with everything you've got; always being open to discovering more, making mistakes, and learning from them.

If you put passion into your work, your relationships, your life, no matter what you do, I want to learn from you.

Towards the end of our days, the only thing we need to analyze to know if we led a **FULFILLED** life is the number of people we inspired and helped along the way. Let's keep inspiring, let's keep helping, let's keep learning. Let's continue leaving a mark!

FULFILLED

A FULFILLING LIFE **IS WITHIN YOUR REACH**

It is said that you only live once,
but the truth is that you only die once
and you live every day.

SIMON COHEN
CAP 08

I felt the breeze on my face as we sailed away from the mainland. A perfect day was about to end. We were returning to Cancun after spending several hours on Isla Mujeres. My wife, daughters, and I had rented a small boat and set out on the trip back, figuring we'd enjoy the sunset at sea.

These had been difficult days for the whole family because my father was facing a serious health crisis that had us all very distressed. It had been nine months since he had had a life-threatening cancerous tumor removed. Despite the surgery, my father's health was still very delicate. My mother, brothers, and I had searched for treatment options all over the world. We were in the hands of the best doctors. However, the situation was dire and we all felt exhausted. Our energy was completely depleted, which is why we decided to take the girls to the beach for few days and unplug for a bit.

That sunset was the perfect ending to a spectacular and magical day. The sea was more turquoise than ever, without a single wave, everything was calm. We had anchored for a couple of hours in Mexico's most crystalline waters. We took the opportunity to swim, sunbathe, and enjoy an exquisite ceviche. The weather was perfect.

I thought about how grateful I am for life and for allowing us to enjoy nature in these difficult times. The idea of this snapshot of happiness haunted me, and at the same time, I had mixed feelings: not only was my dad going through a really hard time, I also thought about all the people who were facing complications in their lives.

Death is the price we have to pay for living. Suffering is the price we have to pay for loving. The deeper this pain is, the more intense the love for the one who leaves.

I wish someone had taught me this as a child. My life would have been easier.

Why do they teach us science and math in school, and not happiness and love? Why do they teach us to visualize ourselves as what we want to become without making us aware of the fact that, one day, we will not be here? Why do we focus on the trivial rather than place importance on understanding death? The day we are born is the day we start dying. This is something inevitable and the more aware we are of it, the more we'll enjoy our ride through this world. We would no longer place so much importance on the ugly stares that offend us for months on end. We wouldn't fight with our loved ones over things that are not worth it. We'd focus our energy on building and giving love, instead of destroying and offending.

The five of us sat on the bow, and as we watched the sun set on the horizon, I said to them: "How I wish this day would last a little longer, I would love to stretch it out even for a couple of hours. I'm having such a good time, I'm so comfortable here with you talking, singing, on this beautiful sea, but how can I be so happy if my dad is suffering right now?" I thought of him as I watched the sun go down, tears began to stream down my face, and I said, “Life is like the sunset. The sun that is setting is like my dad, his flame is going out and no matter how much I want to stop it, no matter how much I try, no matter how much I ask him to stay with me for a little while longer because I want to hug him, because I want to enjoy him, because I want to tell him again how much I love him and how grateful I am to him, it won’t be possible. I can’t control that.”

You could barely glimpse the tiniest wick of flame, the only thing that remained from that sun, which had looked like a brilliant and perfect glowing ball just minutes before. It was slowly fading away. I wanted to grab it, I wanted to pull it towards me and say: “Stay a little bit longer, please, give me one more minute.” But that was impossible! You can’t ask the sun not to set. You can’t ask the world to stop either. That’s how I understood that we can’t tell the people we love to stay a little longer when their time is coming to an end.

Sometimes life hurts, exhausts, aches. It is not perfect, it is not fair, it is not coherent. It is not easy, it is not eternal. In spite of everything, this is life and we have to enjoy it!

That analogy made me understand that, whatever I do, whatever I think, his time will be his. My father’s sunset will come when it has to come, but that light, his light, will continue to shine for many years afterwards within the people who love him. That fire will always be there burning. This is how a new dawn begins, and the next day, the same sun that hid the night before will rise on the other side. No one can avoid it, so we have to enjoy every moment, every instant, every experience.

Night was falling and I couldn't stop thinking about what was to come. We stayed a little longer and that led me to understand that, although of course we were going to put all our efforts into making sure that my father received the best medical care, we'd have to accept the moment when nature said, "That's it!" And I insist, this is going to happen to all of us, whether we like it or not. The only thing we should pray for is that the goodbyes come in chronological order: the young saying goodbye to the old.

At that moment, I compared our life to the day we'd had. We relished and laughed, ate and walked, enjoyed ourselves as a family until the end. That's life! We must take advantage of the sunlight while we have it, the light of our parents when we have them, the light of life, knowing we are lucky enough to breathe, not allow anything to obscure it because the time will come when that beautiful sun will go away. In fact, when we rejoice in a sunset, it is because we know that the sun will be rising again the next day. It's something that happens every day, a miracle, and that afternoon at sea, I had an incredible epiphany.

There is a saying in India that goes: "When a person is born, the baby cries while everyone around him smiles.

When a person dies, he is the one smiling and everyone around him cries." It's part of the lessons that life has given me so far. We must enjoy every moment, be present to seize every second, be at peace with both the good and bad things that make us human.

The price that humans must pay for living and loving, for laughing and enjoying, is to die. And as Mark Twain said:

The fear of death follows from the fear of life. A man who lives fully is prepared to die at any time.

We've all been through or will go through something similar. Now, reflect on my story and put names to the main characters from your own life, look within you, and think about how you experience those difficult moments, or how you will experience them when they happen. If you're at the dawn of a loved one, savor it, live it, enjoy it! Don't miss the opportunity that life is granting you. If you're in the glow and you're not satisfied, react! You only get one chance to live. And if you are at the dusk of a loved one, don't miss the chance to tell him how much you love him and how grateful you are for everything he has done for you. If you wait, it may be too late.

The moment I faced death, I thought I would vanish from this planet and that my turn was up. Life gave me another chance and later, when I had that feeling of enlightenment that changed my way of seeing life forever, I understood that the most valuable things are not bought with money. What truly matters is something we already have and is free. We all have it and can all enjoy it.

Hugging, loving, laughing, or crying. It's up to us how we decide to live our life, whether we stand before it with a smile or with a frown, because true success is based on the attitude with which you face each situation.

With his example of integrity and resilience, my father has taught me that our actions are what define our name and reputation, and our attitude towards life will either bring us closer to or distance us from fulfillment. If that attitude is positive and we have the will to live a happy existence, it will be much easier. In the end, what we are able to obtain will depend on how we take things, to be able to take a step forward and keep fighting for our dreams.

You only live once, but if you do it right, once is enough.

When you understand this, you can be happier and calmer because you know that death is coming. No matter how hard you try, we are all going to move on to that next phase. That's why we have to experience life and find a purpose in order to learn how to die with dignity, to die well, in the best way. The idea is to die 'young', as late as possible.

As the writer Mario Vargas Llosa says: "It's important to be alive until the end, not to die in life, not to lose hope, not to sit down and wait for death. If one manages to live like this to the end, then death is an accident that surprises you when you are still living fully. Life is a wonderful thing and we must try to live it and take advantage of it until the end."

Happiness is born from accepting our vulnerability and knowing that sooner or later we'll be gone. Embracing it allows us to free ourselves and move to another level of consciousness and emotion, free our souls, let go, and acknowledge that the sun, at some point, will set.

Before that sunset at sea, I had not thought of what it meant to die with dignity. Now I think that, when the time comes, when I am closing the final chapter of my story, I'll have to say with all the strength of my soul:

What an incredible life I've had!

Because the day I die, my eyes will close but my heart will remain open forever. Because I don't want to be buried, I want to be planted like a tree that will bear fruit for those who remain in this world!

I'll accept that at that moment my journey will end, and I enjoyed, laughed, cried, and loved deeply. I had many friends, I influenced people in a positive way, I received, I learned, I did not disrespect others, I did not betray my values. I will be at peace. From the bottom of my heart, I hope the same thing happens to you.

The body leaves, but the soul never dies. It is the soul that we must try to fill so that, when our sun goes down, we leave with a full soul.

Learning to live with the full awareness that death is something imminent does not mean that there will be no suffering. There will be, because there is no growth without suffering: it is part of life, it is part of our cycle in this world, it is the circle of life, it is something that leads us to learn, grow, and evolve.

Living is about flourishing as human beings.

It's about growing in every way. We must bloom so that when it is our turn to wither, we do so with dignity.

Sharing your life with others, being empathetic, surrounding yourself with people more capable than yourself, and maintaining a positive attitude –this is the real secret to success, because success is a feeling in the soul, not in a number in a bank account.

To live **FULFILLED** is to be at peace with yourself. That starry night, looking at the sky and hugging my family, I realized that I had everything in order to try to be the happiest man in the world. Yes, the happiest man in the world! All I had to do was make the decision, and take on the commitment and the responsibility. After that, I could live in peace, surrounded by love, **FULFILLED!** Despite all my faults and virtues, despite the problems I face, despite the pain and suffering, being **FULFILLED** is an attitude, and we can all achieve it!

Those of us who have had an encounter with death or with something close to it, something that scares us and that is bigger than us, are forced to be at peace with it in order to determine our next step.

Don't wait for something so extreme to happen to you in order to learn the lesson! A person who learns from other peoples' experiences is intelligent.

Live happily!

LIVE **FULFILLED!**

Do things with integrity and you'll see that your life will be much simpler, because life is short and time goes by very quickly, without reruns, without the possibility of going back.

Enjoy every moment as it comes!

Don't waste your time and energy being angry! Because every minute of anger is 60 seconds less of happiness!

Being **FULFILLED** is to accept that at any moment, we can transcend and feel satisfied with our own lives.

Start writing the story you want to tell towards the end of your days!

Start living and enjoying yourself to the fullest!

Your countdown starts today.

What do you want to do with the rest of your life?

Achieving a fulfilled life is in your hands!

I will be inspired and will continue to learn from others. I will dream of a better world, in peace, surrounded by love. Because love cures it all!

Let's keep building the world we want to leave for our children!

Let's keep smiling, hugging, helping, spreading happiness!

In spite of everything, this is life and we have to enjoy it!

We're going together towards a better tomorrow!

I will live a **FULFILLED** life and nothing and no one can change my mind!

FULFILLED

PHRASE GLOSSARY

This section is designed to be a practical tool for you to use in those moments when you need advice or a positive thought to motivate you.

Keep it on your nightstand and open it up any day of the year.

I'm sure that when you read it, it will help you to make a better roadmap for your personal path.

Chapter 1

We have two lives: the second one begins when we realize we only have one.

When you get what you want, it is life directing you. When you don't get what you want, it is life protecting you.

Everything happens for a reason, for something good, and we only come to understand this as time passes. These are gifts in disguise that life gives us.

Time is one of our most valuable assets.

In order to be someone important, first you have to look like someone important.

When 'success' comes at the expense of your health, your family, or your friends, it's not success.

Life gives us a limited amount of energy each morning and we have the right to choose how and to what ends we use it. In fighting and being destructive, or in building and being creative. It's our choice.

Sometimes, it's better to be at peace than to be right.

To be happy is also to have a good support system.

We came into this world to be happy. The problem is that we forget.

Our pace of life is very fast: it makes us worry about shallow things that eventually become important, and then, what is really important becomes shallow.

Your happiness today cannot depend on something that happened in the past or will happen in the future.

A **FULFILLED** man lives intensely and is ready to transcend at any moment.

Chapter 2

Happiness is the new rich, inner peace is the new success, health is the new wealth, and education, respect, and values are the base for our future.

There are two types of dreamers: the first one dreams in his sleep, at night; the second dreams during the day, and at night he can't sleep.

There's no second chance to make a first impression.

The difference between pain and suffering is that pain is physical and suffering is produced in the mind.

You can't make a bad deal with good people.

There are people so poor, so poor, that all they have is a lot of money.

You can't be happy while hungry or cold, it is what it is.

It's very complicated to find happiness within oneself, but it is impossible to find it anywhere else.

Heaven and hell are not physical places: they are states of mind. When you're at peace, you're in heaven; when you're not, you're in hell.

The day you stop growing is the day you start dying.

We always work for a better tomorrow, but when that tomorrow comes, instead of enjoying it, we again think of a better tomorrow. Let's have a better today and enjoy the present!

To know that you did your best is to be at peace, to come home and sleep in harmony. You can't be at peace if you don't do your job well. Tranquility is the greatest manifestation of happiness. It's that easy.

We have to be aware that when we fall into the depths, it is because down there, there is something to be found, something to be learned.

No one can choose the day they'll die, but we do have the ability to decide what attitude we will face life with.

Let us be happy, not because everything is perfect or fine, but because we are alive and that is reason enough to celebrate.

One is not happy because everything is fine, but because one finds the good in everything.

We have to value and love everything that is ours. Whether it is a lot or a little, it is ours!

Remember when you yearned for what you have today?

Happiness is the difference between your expectations and your reality, between what you want and what you have.

The more you work for something, the more you enjoy it when you get it. If you can go home and sleep soundly, congratulations! You're much closer to happiness than you might have imagined.

Chapter 3

Strive to be so great that everyone wants to be like you, and so humble that everyone wants to be with you.

When nothing changes, if I change, everything changes.

Fear makes you humble.

When you lose, don't miss out on the lesson. If there is a great teacher of life, it is failure.

What is failure? It's not when you don't reach your goal; it's not reaching the goals and not learning from the experience – that's the real failure!

I never lose; I win, or I learn.

When you're tired and don't want to go on, rest, but don't quit!

When your mind is not under control, it is insatiable, like fire: it always wants more.

Happiness is a combination of using your gifts, doing what you like in a disciplined way, and following the rules.

Doing the work you are good at and loving doing it every day - that is not work, it is joy.

Que sera, sera. Whatever will be, will be.

That combination of ambition and humility is what made me dream of being a truly human human being.

Physical preparation is just as important as mental preparation.

To build a road, the first thing you have to think about is where it comes from and where it goes.

Repeating every day what you want to achieve and having the ability to close your eyes and see it, this puts it in your path.

First you have to fill your pockets, save. The surplus is the only thing you can spend.

They say a man's true success is measured by the size of his wife's smile.

When you genuinely care about others, there is a consequence: others will also care about you.

You have to be ambitious, but humble.

Humility is to plant your feet firmly on the ground, no matter the brand of your shoes.

Seeking constant growth must be part of every human being's life, always based on their life purpose.

You must team up with people more talented than you are because, let's face it: there's always something you can learn from others.

We have two ears and one mouth so that we can listen twice as much as we speak.

If you're happy about other people's success, you've got it all figured out!

Being grateful, being humble, being afraid, and being vulnerable all lead to a better connection with people.

Chapter 4.

The best moment to believe in your dreams was when you were a kid. The second best moment is today.

My life has been full of tragedies, 99% of them never happened.

Learning to express and defend my point of view was as important as doing so without offending anyone.

Every action has a consequence, so before you do anything, think about the future.

The more I praise my people, the more I praise myself.

Don't wait until your loved ones are gone to miss them and thank them; if you are one of the lucky ones who still has them with you, call them right now and tell them how much you love them!

The best way to find yourself is to lose yourself in the service of others.

When two people think alike, one of them is redundant.

Empathy is being able to see for a moment with your own eyes what others are feeling; it is the possibility of sitting in the other's chair and trying to understand their vision, to find points of agreement, and to start building from there.

Respect is the right of others to think differently than you.

Let's stop buying our children what we never had and start teaching them everything we learned. The essential is invisible.

It's okay to NOT be okay; it's part of being human.

Chapter 5.

Do what is difficult and your life will be easy; do what is easy and your life will be difficult.

You can't teach if you're not willing to learn and do so constantly.

The future belongs to those who learn, unlearn, and relearn.

If you don't say, "I behaved so foolishly a year ago," you didn't learn enough this year.

Our company is successful because we decided to be happy and work on this every day. Success is a consequence of being happy.

If you're not happy with everything you have, you won't be happy with everything you lack either. We need to learn to want what we have and not have what we want.

Being happy also means having the patience and self-esteem to accept that not every day will be a happy day.

Everything happens for a good reason, although many times we may not understand that reason in the moment. Time needs to pass in order for us to discover the treasure that life has given us.

Let's control what we can, and what we can't, let the universe fix it.

What brought us to where we are will not take us to where we dream of going.

Complaining brings scarcity, gratitude brings abundance.

In order to be successful, and above all to be happy, gratitude is key.

Sometimes people turn against you, and that helps you grow towards being a better human. If we understand it that way, it's a great way to help yourself.

Sometimes you win by losing and there's no way to fail if you give it your all.

Leaders who don't listen will eventually be surrounded by people who have nothing to say.

The person who asks may look foolish for a minute; the person who does not ask will be foolish all his life.

You are never too important to not be nice to people.

Diversity is our strength.

Integrity is doing the right thing even when no one is watching.

What is right is right even if no one does it, and what is wrong is wrong even if everyone does it.

Honesty is about your outwards actions: what I do, what I say, my public actions. Integrity is doing the right thing even when no one is watching: who I am, what I think, and my private actions.

Your example as a leader should inspire others to be humble, while you continue to be the leader of a team with big goals and ambition.

A mistake that makes you humble is much more valuable than an achievement that makes you arrogant.

Nothing in nature lives for itself. The rivers do not drink their own water; the trees do not eat their own fruit; the sun does not shine on itself and flowers do not spread their fragrance for themselves. Living for others is a rule of nature. We are all born to help each other. No matter how difficult it is... Life is good when you are happy; but much better when others are happy because of you.

Everything can be taken from a man but one thing: the last of the human freedoms—to choose one's attitude in any given set of circumstances, to choose one's own way.

We all have problems. There is not a person on the planet who does not have them. We came to this planet to solve them.

Once, a person who had a serious accident was asked, "How can you be so positive after losing your legs?" He replied, "How can you be so negative when you have both of yours?"

Remember that from time to time, not getting what you want is a tremendous stroke of luck!

You can't connect the dots by looking forward; you can only do it by looking backward. So, you have to trust that they will connect positively in some way in the future.

Neither all the joy nor all the sadness.

Walking on the path to happiness does not just mean that you want to be happy; happiness is achieved when you make others feel good.

In business, as in life, it all comes down to how you make people feel. It's that easy and that hard.

The most human enterprise will be the most successful.

Henco is a happiness company that also happens to work in logistics.

The bottom line is that we want to be happy, and that should be the rule, not the exception.

How we use that energy is up to us. You decide whether you use it to build a full life and transmit it to others, or use it to fight, argue, offend, and destroy.

Let's transform the energy that life gives us into positive things because this is real life! We don't have another one; life is not a rehearsal.

Chapter 6.

No matter how educated, talented, rich or powerful you are, the way you treat people says it all.

You can't be happy when you're hungry or cold; the better you perform, the happier you are, and the happier you are, the better you perform. It's a virtuous circle.

It is practically impossible to have a fulfilled life if you are not happy in your work.

Be a flexible company while maintaining control.

Everyone is fighting a battle that you know nothing about, so ALWAYS be kind.

You learn from everything if you are alert to the messages that life sends!

If you want to go fast, go alone, if you want to go far, go with others.

Life is too short to be happy only on the weekend.

Having happy employees means having satisfied customers and, consequently, positive results.

People do not decide their future, they decide their habits, and their habits define their future.

If you have stability in your personal life, you can be stable in your work life.

Doing intense and fun work with the best attitude will make you truly happy.

Our goal is to be the best at what we do and to spread happiness.

The hours you spend sleeping are an investment, every minute you put into it gives a return of two minutes of the best version of you.

Stop trying to calm the storm. Find your own calm, give your best, and the storm will pass.

Sometimes the secret to being at peace is having a bad memory.

They say that a person is intelligent if they learn from others' mistakes.

When you focus on the good, the good becomes extraordinary.

High performance is something we can teach; being happy with what you do is the consequence.

When people are happy, they can work miracles.

The best way to learn is wanting to do so.

Happiness is the new rich, inner peace is the new success, health is the new wealth, and education, respect, and values are the coolest thing ever!

Being polite is what is most valued, we have to make it trendy!

Chapter 7.

You don't build a business. You build the people, and then the people build the business.

The way you react in your most difficult moments defines how you make your way to success.

The world breaks everyone and afterward many are strong at the broken places.

Making sense of what you do changes the way you look at things.

Logistics can be very stressful if you don't put heart into it. We do logistics with a human touch.

If you use real actions to prove to your team that you are going to take care of them, without a doubt they'll reciprocate.

When one teaches, two learn.

The biggest difference between money and time, is that you can know how much money you have, but you will never know how much time you have left.

If you focus on helping others grow, you grow. If you focus on the problems, the problems grow.

The people who love you will have the courage to point out your flaws, and the patience to help you correct them.

Everyone smiles in the same language.

A smile costs nothing but gives much. It enriches those who receive it without making poorer those who give it. It takes but a moment, but the memory of it sometimes lasts forever.

A smile is a weapon that disarms.

The people who smile the most are not always those with the least problems, but the ones who manage to see the good things more than or in spite of the bad ones.

Technology brings us closer to those who are far away and distances us from those who are near.

A smile is still the best garnish in any conversation.

There are three stages in becoming a good leader: the first is to give your best; the second is to learn that when you are present, you bring out the best version of your teammates; and the third is that this behavior prevails in your absence.

Passion is incredibly contagious, it produces wonderful energy. Passion is not a state of mind, but a way of being.

Leaders must have a service-driven attitude, be down-to-earth, and have as their ultimate goal the creation and training of more leaders.

Think three times as much, listen twice as much, and talk half as much.

Triumph is not for the one who knows best, but for the one who surrounds himself with the best companions.

Our differences, aptly used, make us stronger.

Every person who crosses my path is better at something than I am, and it's a passion for me to find out what that thing is.

I don't like that man. I must get to know him better.

If, by asking for others' opinion we seek only applause, no one grows.

Challenges are born from frustrations.

Acknowledging others is one of the easiest ways to approach them.

If you surround yourself with five reliable people, you will be the sixth; if you surround yourself with five intelligent people, you will be the sixth; if you surround yourself with five fulfilled people, you will be the sixth; if you surround yourself with five negative people, you will be the sixth.

If you put passion into your work, your relationships, your life, no matter what you do, I want to learn from you.

Chapter 8.

It is said that you only live once, but the truth is that you only die once and you live every day.

Death is the price we have to pay for living. Suffering is the price we have to pay for loving. The deeper this pain is, the more intense the love for the one who leaves.

The day we are born is the day we start dying.

Sometimes life hurts, exhausts, aches. It is not perfect, it is not fair, it is not coherent. It is not easy, it is not eternal. In spite of everything, this is life and we have to enjoy it!

When a person is born, the baby cries while everyone around him smiles. When a person dies, he is the one smiling and everyone around him cries.

The fear of death follows from the fear of life. A man who lives fully is prepared to die at any time.

You only live once, but if you do it right, once is enough.

The idea is to die 'young', as late as possible.

It's important to be alive until the end, not to die in life, not to lose hope, not to sit down and wait for death. If one manages to live like this to the end, then death is an accident that surprises you when you are still living fully. Life is a wonderful thing and we must try to live it and take advantage of it until the end.

Because the day I die, my eyes will close but my heart will remain open forever.

There is no growth without suffering.

Living is about flourishing as human beings.

We must bloom so that when it is our turn to wither, we do so with dignity.

Success is a feeling in the soul, not in a number in a bank account.

FULFILLED

APPENDIX

SIMON COHEN

Most people are born, live, and die without knowing why they exist. Simon Cohen faced death, and this was the greatest gift he received in life. It was an awakening to a new level of consciousness.

Before, he understood like many that success depended on external achievements, on accumulating and getting what you want or, in other words, seeking what you are not. The event in Hong Kong generated a profound change in him early in his life, and a change in his idea of what his business, Henco, should be.

He discovered the true meaning of two words that we tend to use interchangeably: success and happiness. This book, aptly titled **FULFILLED,** is the story of a life, as well as a practical and insightful reflection for those who are in search of meaning, purpose, and finding happiness. Simon teaches us that happiness is closer than we think it is, and that it is an attitude that only occurs in the present, in the today and the now, enjoying what we are and what we have. A must read.

Salvador Alva

Former President of Tecnológico de Monterrey and PepsiCo Latin America

ooo

What an honor to have the opportunity to express some words about a unique person, my dear friend Simon Cohen! A true gentleman, whom I consider a visionary who inspired me immensely.

Without a doubt, he has built a wonderful and solid business. And, most importantly, he managed to take his company to another level by keeping all the staff together as one big family, without sacrificing productivity. As we all know, his motto in life is happiness and, in fact, he manages to spread this feeling to everyone around him.

Through his philosophy, Simon established a unique workplace environment. He managed to instill a positive spirit in his team, and promoted good health as a way of life, creating a virtuous circle both at home and in the office. This is true balance!

I firmly believe that all his achievements are the essence and result of the strong values he learned from his wonderful parents. I feel privileged to be a part of this book, dedicated to an extraordinary man, his father!

Diego Aponte
President at MSC Group

ooo

I was fortunate enough to meet Simon ten years ago, and I say fortunate because not only did I meet him, but we have become very close friends since then. Being in the same YPO forum has allowed us to get to know each other as if we were brothers.

Simon is the most transparent person I've ever met: he doesn't hide anything. Full of dreams, concerns, fears, energy, but most of all, a lot of love for others, he cares and is concerned about helping those around him.

If you ask him for a favor, he does it immediately and makes sure that he has completely sorted out what you needed. He is a very well-connected person and uses these relationships to support anyone who needs it.

When Simon told me about the awards that Henco had received for taking care of its people, I was not surprised at all. If he cares about his family and friends as he does about his team at Henco, it wasn't surprising at all if his company was acknowledged as a great place to work. I am convinced that the basis of Henco's success is Simon's leadership and the motivation he has extended to his employees. They go full speed ahead and without stress; a true success story of a fast-growing company with a motivated and happy team.

High Performance, Happy People is not something that had to be created at Henco; it came naturally, and it was enough to put a name to what had happened thanks to Simon's leadership.

I'm sure this book will be useful to anyone who wants to learn that success and happiness are not easy to achieve, but that with a positive attitude, nothing is impossible. Sometimes people think it's a matter of luck – but as we can see in Simon and his family's story, Henco resulted from effort, intense work, and knowing how to create real teams, both within the family and in the company.

Simon clearly knows that his main enterprise is his family, and that's why he has taken such good care of his parents, of his relationships with his siblings, of being a good husband, and of being a great example for his daughters. Without a doubt, his goal is for those who work at Henco to be successful and happy. That's what really makes him feel **FULFILLED.**

Eduardo Coronado
CEO of Coflex

ooo

It was a warm winter morning in November 2015. I distinctly remember the moment when the work group detected and then made explicit what Simon had been experiencing and absorbing from the core of Henco's organization. High Performance, Happy People was born and now echoes in the hearts, minds, and words of many.

This has not only influenced the people who work at Henco, but all those who interact with Simon. It is unavoidable to feel this powerful vibration.

I am very proud of Simon and his team, and more importantly, I feel blessed and privileged to have walked part of this journey together.

Simon is constantly thinking about being disruptive to his own processes, because if he doesn't, someone else will. That's the right way to do it.

This book is full of those disruptive ideas that derive from this simple but profound value. Let's enjoy!

Sunil Dovedy
Main Associate, Adizes Institute Worldwide

○○○

It's hard not to be affected by Simon's energy and good vibe. The first reaction is one of reserve. One cannot believe that someone goes through life, at all times, radiating such happiness. However, you soon come to realize the origin of such a quest for full happiness, and how it becomes a life mission to transmit to everyone you meet along the way.

I strongly relate to Simon because I agree that teams, and people in general, respond differently when you care about them in an authentic and genuine way. It's true that happiness is contagious. As entrepreneurs, we have to make sure that our teams are motivated every morning to turn off the alarm clock, jump out of bed, and come to work. The difficult thing is to get people motivated on a daily basis and permanently, and that's basically what Simon has achieved at Henco.

I believe that the greatest learning process for transnational companies lies in establishing a personalized treatment of its employees, caring for others to the smallest detail, and making people happy at work in order to achieve the highest performance and success. I love that Henco's concept goes one step further and focuses on making customers, suppliers, and their families happy too. In the end, we owe it to them, and they need to be at the center of what we do.

I agree with Simon: as leaders, we have to act with integrity, learn to be vulnerable, and always be grateful and humble. This is what allows us to listen and learn from others in order to continue growing. As Simon says: we must seek to be **FULFILLED** in order to transcend. Without regret, we are here to give it our all! To seek our own happiness, to make others happy, and to achieve inner peace.

Alberto de la Fuente
President and CEO of Shell México

ooo

Simon is an extraordinary person. Several people, including my family, have told me that he is very pleasant, enthusiastic, positive, and proactive.

I've had the privilege of being in a lot of meetings and going on trips with him over the last 18 years. I have witnessed the amazing trajectory of his company's growth. There is a lot to learn from him: the way he treats his people, his capacity for work, and his way of relating to others. An honest, emotional, always well-meaning individual, without expecting anything in return. That's my friend Simon Cohen!

Rodrigo González Calderón
CEO at Grupo Gonher

ooo

On a routine business trip to Mexico in January 2010, my colleagues informed me that the last meeting before returning home would be at the airport with a local freight forwarder named Henco. I had never heard of Henco before, let alone its owner Simon Cohen, so I didn't have high expectations. As we introduced ourselves, Simon greeted me with a big hug, as if we were old friends.

What I remember most about that first meeting with Simon was his passion, his positive energy, and his simplicity. Who would have thought that this first meeting would be the beginning of a great friendship? Simon is now one of my closest friends, a person I admire. I am very grateful to have him in my life.

For the past ten years, I have had the joy of personally knowing not only Simon, but also his late father, brothers, and the Henco family – and learning from them all. One common denominator that I have witnessed firsthand in the Cohen family and at Henco is integrity and incredible empathy for other people. In the business environment, Simon calls it High Performance, Happy People. I would call it a truly unique human experience.

In the corporate world, where cynicism and short-term profits are usually the priority, it is amazing and inspiring to witness leadership like Simon's, challenging convention, built on true values, and founded on personal integrity.

Together with his brothers, Simon has created an exemplary company, which is permeated by a feeling of family and a personal commitment to the employees.

For the past three years, I have had the honor of serving on Henco's Board of Advisors. This has allowed me to get to know Simon and Henco even better, and to witness the personal journey that Simon has embarked upon to reinvent himself, leading from behind the scenes and entering a new role as Chief Visionary Officer at Henco. On many occasions, I have probably been his fiercest critic, but it has always been pure, honest, and born of my admiration and affection for him and his project.

Playing a small part in this journey and being a part of Simon's life is and will continue to be an incredible experience and a true honor for me.

Michael Hansen
Former Global Sales Director of Maersk Line and member of Henco's Global Board of Advisors

ooo

I would like to begin with a phrase from Simon's book: "Everything happens for a good reason that sometimes we cannot understand because we need time." I met a very young Simon who knew nothing about the logistics industry, but was so eager to learn that he always surprised me. What he set out to do, he actually accomplished.

I was fortunate enough to meet a great human being who always, up until the final day of our partnership, treated us with love and loyalty. What he has achieved deserves nothing but my respect and admiration.

Our paths took different directions in 2007. Manfred and I constantly talk about Simon's qualities as a human being and entrepreneur. We have maintained a sincere friendship with mutual respect. I am grateful for the beautiful words expressed in this book about me and about Manfred; they reflect the great person that Simon is.

Congratulations, Simoncito, I congratulate you with all my heart. You are a great man, a great human being – never change!

Thomas Kröger
Mentor, Business Advisor and Former Partner

I met Simon in the spring of 1997 when we were looking to find a representative in Monterrey for our international logistics company. Simon had only recently graduated from Tec de Monterrey and was working in the family business. He was a young man, my children's age, and I was impressed by his determination and tenacity to want to undertake something of his own and not be dependent on his father's wallet. In spite of his lack of knowledge and experience in our line of business, he seemed to me to be the ideal candidate, and shortly afterwards, he would become our partner in the Monterrey branch.

Somehow, I think we were both convinced that this combination of youth and dynamism with experience and confidence was going to lead us to a good place. We were not wrong, and although years later our paths diverged, to this day I can proudly say that Simon has become not only my best student and friend, but also an extraordinary businessman who has succeeded in becoming the teacher!

Today, Henco is one of the best companies to work for. Hats off to my friend, Simon.

Manfred Jaekel

Former partner, mentor, and friend

Simon is synonymous with life, joy, and positivity. It is finding the how you 'can' overcome all the challenges that are presented to you. Henco is an organization made by people and for people, and this can be seen in the obsession with excellence in customer service that characterizes them. It is not necessary to know what the philosophy behind it is: you experience it in every interaction with any member of the Henco team.

Happiness is an attitude, it is a declaration that one makes to the world. It can be implemented as a lifestyle, or it can be configured as we move forward along the path. Nobody is perfect, but if we know that we want to declare ourselves as happy people, we will always be aware and focused on achieving it.

Essentially, happiness is the remainder between expectations and reality, so it is vital to know how to establish expectations and create, with our thoughts and actions realities that contribute positively to the formula.

Emilio Lozano Cavazos
Board President of Grupo Forem

ooo

A friend is a person we know we can always count on and who is always present. That is what my friendship with Simon is like, and I value it immensely.

When you told me, Simon, that you gave lectures about happiness, and people approached you afterwards to congratulate you, often with tears in their eyes, I couldn't believe it. Some years ago, we traveled to

Seattle, where I had the opportunity to hear you speak for the first time. Since then, I have seen you in various forums, and you surprise me more and more. After reading **FULFILLED**, I can confirm that, using your concepts, people see situations and moments of their own lives reflected. This gives them a different perspective on something that they always had in front of them, but that they had never really seen before.

You have changed so many people's way of living and thinking by helping them become better parents, children, siblings, partners, and in general, better people. The way you teach people to always see the good in every situation is admirable.

This book is the reflection of a person who, through effort, dedication, and love, managed to grow and transmit the happiness and fullness that we ought to have in life. Congratulations!

Saúl Mugrabi

Brother-in-law, friend, and life mentor

ooo

I have known Simon since I was seven years old, and I know first-hand the top-quality kind of human being he is. No one has to tell me about it. I know him as he is, and I can proudly declare to you that he is a **FULFILLED** human being, just like he depicts in his excellent book! **FULFILLED** because he is honest, helpful, but above all loyal and committed to always helping those around him.

Simon, like everyone else, has strengths and weaknesses. One of his great virtues is the tool of visualization. When swimming, he used this great virtue to plan his competition: he saw it and lived it just as he was going to execute it in the pool. And his mind, more than his body, led him to achieve what he had visualized so many times in order to fulfill his goals. He still does this – only now he is doing it in his professional and personal life.

Simon is very passionate and has a winning spirit that drives him to give his best. His mind leads him to always give that extra something to fulfill his goals. I believe his passion and heart have taken him even further! That continues to manifest itself in him success as an entrepreneur, as well as a husband, son, and friend.

Simon doesn't do it alone. He leads his team along the way. With his joy, optimism, and attitude, he encourages those around him to give their all, so that everyone achieves their goals. He is a great motivator, who brings out the best in the people around him. When he reaches the final goal, he is very grateful and always celebrates the achievements with others.

I highly recommend reading this book so that you can be as lucky as I am to be a grain of sand in Simon's great story, because, during our friendship, he has helped me be a better person. Thank you for everything, Simon!

Juan Carlos Puente

President for the North Latin American Region, Whirlpool Corporation

ooo

It is impossible for me to express in words what I have learned from reading **FULFILLED**, as well as how grateful I am to Simon for having shared with me his way of life, his beliefs, and practices. The text is extraordinary, full of extraordinary riches for the reader. As I read it, I was reminded again of several conversations we've had and of conferences of his in which I have been present, which are a delight and an opportunity for continuous learning. Thank you, thank you, and thank you very much, dear Simon.

In **FULFILLED**, Simon, in a totally transparent and generous way, shares with us his life's vision and the conviction that our purpose in this world is to seek others' happiness, as well as our own. What has been achieved at Henco – High Performance, Happy People – is a true reflection of Simon's thinking, sayings, and actions in his daily life, both personally and professionally. I have seen the importance, the transcendence, and the benefits for people and for organizations, of orienting their actions towards human beings, their wellbeing and happiness. As a business leader or as an individual, we must all take advantage of this great work, full of values and practical wisdom, to become better, to inspire and help those around us in this cause, and to transcend. Whether you require a reboot, as Simon did, or you have already advanced on the road to happiness, in **FULFILLED** you will find a series of concepts that will help guide your actions in building towards this great purpose, that of being happy. Thank you, Simon, for the invitation you extend to us in this book to be **FULFILLED.** We gladly accept it. Reading this book has inspired me again, and has helped, once more, in my journey towards happiness.

Ricardo Saldívar

Former President and CEO of The Home Depot México

ooo

I am proud to have the privilege of writing a few words about Simon, his life philosophy and him as a person. I feel very fortunate to consider him one of the closest people in my life, both personally and as a family member, and even in business.

A close relationship works when there is mutual admiration between two people. I have great respect for Simon because of his unique and incomparable way of being.

Outside of the family circle, I have spent more time with him and his family in the last few years, and I can really see that what he writes in these pages about what he thinks and the way he acts on a daily basis, is the way he handles his relationships in what he does. He is 100% authentic. This is really how he is as an individual, which reflects the essence of his spirit.

Every time I see Simon, he radiates an extraordinary light. It is rare to see a person so illuminated by happiness and inner peace. I don't know anyone who genuinely cares more about others than they do about themselves, as Simon does.

His nature of serving others has brought him great gifts: a beautiful family, successful businesses, and countless friends, as he develops deep and lasting connections with each person he meets.

For all these reasons, I am convinced that we can all learn from Simon's philosophy. I consider him an exceptional being. **FULFILLED** shows us the way to achieve the happiness we all seek.

Simon, keep being you. Thank you for sharing your experience with us. I know this book will bring enormous benefits to anyone who reads it. My respect, love, and admiration, always.

Mauricio Schwarz
CEO of Brochas y Productos

ooo

I am lucky to have known Simon since childhood. I have watched closely your achievements, your clashes with life, and your successful way of running a business, where you have the deep conviction that happiness is an integral part of the lives of all the people you work with and know.

You have managed to tattoo happiness onto your family, your employees, your friends, and that was one of the reasons why I invited you to join the Tecmilenio University Board, where for some years now we have been exploring the topic of the ecosystem of happiness, wellbeing, and health. Your participation has been extremely valuable, and you have left a deep mark on this university.

Furthermore, I want to tell you that we could be soulmates in this life journey, because of the similar health difficulties and circumstances we have been through.

As a cancer and heart surgery survivor, my positive attitude has greatly influenced my ability to overcome the challenges that life has put before me, while allowing me to enjoy it to the fullest. Today I feel very fortunate to enjoy good health, success in business, and feel **FULFILLED.**

Simon, as you say in your book, money can buy material things, but it cannot buy time! So, every minute is something very precious that life gives us, and we should take advantage of it and enjoy this marvel that we call life.

My most sincere congratulations for all your achievements, your generosity, and for always being a great friend.

Miguel Schwarz Marx

Businessman, mentor, and friend

ooo

I was fortunate enough to meet Simon through YPO. When I met him, he was a young, vibrant young man, who showed in his way of expressing himself a love and passion for what he was doing.

Across 20 years of sharing experiences, I have realized that this energy of an Olympic athlete is imprinted in all his projects with a distinctive, intelligent, and bold vision.

For a person who is so busy and has so many things going on, it is difficult to achieve a balance between work and family. However, Simon has the ability to harmonize and balance enjoying family life, being an entrepreneur, a father, and an exemplary husband.

Ricardo Villarreal
CEO of Imagen Dental

The production of this book was
finished in Mexico City in May 2021
by Tack Boutique Editorial.
www.tack.mx

FULFILLED